The construction of a new profession

WITHDRAWN
FROM STOCK

THE CONSTRUCTION OF A NEW PROFESSION

*A European perspective on professionalism in
Early Childhood Education and Care*

Jan Peeters

uitgeverij
SWP

With the support of the Bernard van Leer Foundation

Bernard van Leer *Foundation*

ESF: helping to develop employment by promoting employability, entrepreneurship, adaptability and equal opportunities and by investing in human resources.

VESOC

childcare in learning networks

EQUAL

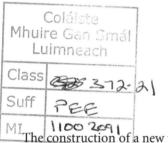
The construction of a new profession

A European perspective on professionalism in Early Childhood Education and Care

Jan Peeters

Translated by Sandy Reijnhart

ISBN 978 90 6665 950 6

NUR 847

INDEX

Foreword

In this study, a comparative overview is given of the professionalization of the childcare professions in England, France, New Zealand and Denmark. The basis of the study is twofold. The first principle is the determination of a paradox in the professionalization of childcare: while the childcare professions are being forced to deal with ever-higher requirements in professionalism, the reality in many countries is very different. This certainly also applies to the situation in Flanders and Belgium, where there is a strong tendency towards deprofessionalization in the childcare sector. The second basic principle is the approach to professionalism as not simply a question of training, but primarily a question of interpretative negotiation and vision development among parents, staff members and policy-makers in childcare.

In this overview, a number of fundamental questions for the debate on professionalization in the childcare sector have been mapped out. One basic question concerns the social function of childcare: what role does childcare play in parenting? Is childcare seen chiefly as residual support for the parents or is it a social right in the support of children and parents in their developmental opportunities, in learning to investigate and understand the world in which we live and in learning to make responsible choices when taking their part in the modeling of their world? In the light of this fundamental question, the debate on professionalism in childcare is essentially based on respect and space for the meaning-making of parents and children. It also encompasses the willingness to investigate one's own actions from the perspective of whether or not these actions contribute to the possibility to realize and negotiate the meaning-making of parents and children. Professionalism in childcare cannot, therefore, be reduced to a debate concerning the rapport between supply and demand; it is principally a debate concerning the on-going and mutual encounter among professionals, parents and children, and on how this encounter can be given a concrete form. The comparative overview presented here demonstrates that encounters depend on clear choices concerning the place of childcare in social policy. There are no magic formulas: the integration of childcare into either the educational policy or the welfare policy provides a positive impulse to the necessary professionalization, yet does not, per definition, provide the positive impulse to the professionalization that the childcare sector needs. In order to do this, it is essential that each country, or each region, carefully works out which possibilities and limitations are inherent in one's own history and how these possibilities can be included and the limitations can be can be exceeded.

Professionalism in childcare encompasses various dimensions: the professionalization of the staff members, of the activities and of the organizations. These dimensions cannot be separated from each other but can only be understood in their mutual interaction. The professionalization of the staff members means that choices are made with respect to the level of training, including the possibilities to allow the short-schooled access to the training courses via alternative learning paths. The professionalization of the staff members must also mean that staff members have the possibility for mobility, both vertically through the influx into higher functions and horizontally through the influx into other functions in the sector. The professionalization of the activities means that training courses must be developed in close relation to the reflection on the practice that is being developed, based on the question of whether or not these practices can (or must) be done differently. It encompasses the precondition of a non-biased look at how a connection can be made between the development of children and the social developments that fundamentally influence the actual childcare sector. One current central point of special attention here is learning to deal with diversity: intercultural activities and gender-neutral training courses also prove to be a stimulus for a more effective professionalism. The professionalization of the organizations means that the image of childcare is an inclusive one, where the diversity of children and parents, but also the diversity of the types of care, are present. One point of attention is therefore, in particular, the situation of the family day carers who, in fact, occupy an important place yet, for many reasons, are not well-represented in the debate on professionalization. The professionalization of the organizations encompasses, moreover, a clear choice to take an extremely critical look at the privatization of the childcare sector, because the consequences for both the quality and the sustainability of the childcare initiatives demand a focused policy, also with respect to the commercial initiatives.

This study is part of a wider study on professionalism in the childcare sector, set up by the author within the framework of his doctorate in Pedagogical Sciences. In this wider study, the practice in the childcare sector is central: the co-construction of a pedagogy of childcare by parents, children, professionals and policy-makers. This comparative overview shows us that this striving for the co-construction of a pedagogy of childcare is not an isolated event, but an international endeavor in which actors from various countries are deeply involved. I sincerely hope that this study contributes to more scope for poli-cymaking and respect for this endeavor by acknowledging the professionalization of the childcare sector as an essential agenda item in the area of social policy and in the social-political choice for an open and democratic society.

Prof. Maria Bouverne-De Bie
Head of the Department of Social Welfare Studies, Ghent University.

Preface of the author

A research question often originates from a feeling of indignation that arises from something that the researcher experiences as unjust, dangerous or unethical. For decades, I and many of my colleagues have been extremely concerned about a dominating discussion that has been going on within the childcare sector of the Flemish Community in Belgium. Politicians, media, labor unions, employers' organizations and a large portion of the public opinion are convinced that there is no preliminary training necessary to be able to care for young children (0 to 3 years old). The necessary expansion of Flemish daycare is being realized at a great pace with short-schooled workers, the majority of whom are – without any type of preliminary training whatsoever – being given the responsibility for very young children.

This has led to a policy paradox within the Flemish childcare sector: although the quality requirements for childcare facilities that have been set by the central government and the parents have increased sharply over the past 30 years, this has not led to setting higher diploma requirements. Quite the reverse is true; only 25% of the employees who work with the children have a diploma or a certificate while, 30 years ago, a diploma was required for every job in childcare.

This policy paradox has also not escaped the attention of the OECD. In the latest report, the OECD (2006) suggests that there is a general consensus among policy-makers and researchers concerning the fact that an upgrading of competencies in the childcare sector is essential, but they acknowledge that this tendency is not being followed in Flanders.

The book that you now have in your hands is part of a PhD dissertation that was set up within the Department of Social Welfare of the Ghent University, after the declaration of this policy paradox concerning professionalism in the childcare sector in Flanders. In order to discover an explanation for this 'deprofessionalization' of childcare within the Flemish Community of Belgium, we have done an analysis of visions and interpretations of parents and policy-makers from the 1970s up to the present day. When planning this study, we asked ourselves whether or not this policy paradox was also taking place in other countries and if there were countries who had found a solution to the paradox. Starting with the Equal-project 'ecce ama! childcare in learning networks', supported by the European Social Fund and the Flemish Community, we were given the opportunity to study this research question within the transnational partnership 'Improving Child-care'. The study of professionalism in the occupations dealing with young children in seven European countries and New Zealand was such an exciting adventure that we have decided to publish our findings in a separate book.

This study would not have been possible without the active support of colleagues from the countries we studied. We thank the partners of 'Improving Childcare', the 14 academics and training experts from France, Germany, Denmark, Luxemburg, Italy, England, the French Community of Belgium and New-Zealand who were prepared to be interviewed on the professionalism of the occupations dealing with young children in their countries. A particular word of thanks goes to Prof. Linda Miller, professor at the Open University and member of the Special Interest Group on Professionalism of EECERA who helped us find our way through the study of the complex English system and who was also prepared to read our text on England. In order to study the situation in France, we called upon the expertise of Myriam Mony, director of the bachelor's training course for *Educateur Jeunes Enfants* (ESSSE-Lyon); for Denmark, the text was read through by Stig Lund, editor-in-chief of the Danish version of the journal 'Children in Europe,' and, for New Zealand, by Karl Le Quesne, Senior Manager Education Management, Ministry of Education of New Zealand and Prof. Carmen Dalli, Victoria University of Wellington. A sincere word of thanks for Prof. Peter Moss, Thomas Coram Institute of the University of London for the critical proofreading of the entire text and for the constructive additions.

This study was part of a PhD thesis and I retain the very best of memories of the inspiring way in which the members of the thesis committee, Prof. Dr. Tonia Aelterman, Prof. Dr. Geert Van Hove, Prof. Freddy Mortier and Prof. Frank Simon have reflected on my work.

In conclusion, a very sincere word of thanks to my thesis supervisor, Prof. Maria De Bie, who convinced me to start this adventure in the first place. The mentoring discussions that we had over the past three years have been exceptionally inspiring for me.

A last word of thanks to the Bernard van Leer Foundation and more in particular to Rita Swinnen, for the support in making the publication of this book possible.

We hope that this book can contribute to the support of a process of professionalization in those countries where the care for the youngest children is still being done by employees who do not possess the required competencies and who are, moreover, forced to work under unfavorable conditions. This study has shown that there is a broad consensus that, in order to give children the chances they are entitled to, a well-trained workforce is essential. The examples from, in particular, Denmark and New Zealand, make it clear that it is possible to construct a democratic professionalism, in which reflective practitioners can manage complex relationships.

Jan Peeters

Ghent, 08.04.08

1

Introduction

The European Union wants to combat the effects of the aging population by creating complete employment. In order to achieve this, the combination of work and family must be made easier. However, for the European Union, childcare is not only seen as a prerequisite for employment, but also as a source of employment. In addition to wanting to create further jobs, the EU has emphasized the importance of these jobs being of 'good quality.' Work must be made more attractive for more people. In other words: Europe wants to create not only more – but also better – jobs in the childcare sector. Quality employment is central to the EU's objective of becoming a knowledge-based economy (European Commission, 2001).

Within the scientific community, there is a consensus on the fact that quality childcare in the early years has a positive effect on the development of the child. In order to create a basis for 'good quality childcare', it is necessary 'to create a sustainable workforce, with the competencies and knowledge to deliver services of high quality'.

There is a growing consensus within Europe regarding the necessity of improving professionalism in the childcare sector. However, there is no agreement regarding how this improvement should occur. The aim of this study is to better define the concept of professionalism in the professions dealing with young children.

The overview of the scientific literature in the first part of this study shows that the professionalization of individuals is a learning process in which, again and again, meaning is given to the interpretation of the profession and which is continually done in relationship to others: the colleagues, the parents and the children.

In light of this, the professionalization process can be seen as a social practice that is the consequence of interaction between, on the one hand, social evolutions, policy measures and new scientific insights and, on the other hand, the researchers, the staff at childcare centres and the parents and the children.

The second part of the study focuses on the gender aspect. Caring for children is still seen in many member states as 'women's work'. Research clearly links this gender-biased concept of professionalism to poor salaries and low qualifications. A new concept of professionalism in care work with young children must be based on a gender-neutral concept. The presence of male staff members and the active involvement of fathers in the facilities are essential conditions for achieving a gender-neutral structure of professionalism. After all, gender-neutral professionalism can only develop through critical consideration and discussion between the male and the female staff members and with the fathers and mothers.

The third part of the study will give an overview of professionalism in care work for young children in various EU countries and New Zealand. This analysis includes the results of a European transnational project which worked on the subject of professionalism in the professions for young children. In this transnational co-operation within the EQUAL-project 'Improving Childcare', financed by the European Social Fund organisations from the French and Flemish Communities of Belgium, Luxembourg, Italy, Germany and Lithuania took part in this EQUAL project. These countries are currently involved in a process of professionalization, but the governments of these countries have not, as yet, outlined a coherent policy regarding the manner in which this professionalism is to be constructed. Our study has shown that Flanders is counteracting this evolution: for the past 25 years, the Flemish childcare sector has been undergoing a process of deprofessionalization.

A more detailed study of childcare was initiated in four countries, selected because (according to the international surveys) they have developed an 'interesting practice and policy' with regard to professionalism.

The study concludes that the integration of childcare (0 to 3 and 4-year olds) into a broader whole (education or 'social welfare activities') has given rise to a process of professionalization (the demand for higher education and higher salaries).

In most EU-countries, there has been a tendency towards establishing bachelor level training courses. These graduates are assisted by less-qualified personnel who generally have a secondary education.

The bachelor-level training courses in France, Denmark and New Zealand – and a number of 'Early Years Foundation Degrees' in England - train students to be reflective practioners, who must be capable of constructing practical, new knowledge.

In these countries, we see methods develop in which the analysis of practices steers the learning process (reflective practice cycle, *analyse de pratiques*). In the training courses in

France and Denmark, this is taken a step further by also including the coaching of less-qualified workers in the curriculum of the bachelor training course.

In some Member States, unqualified workers from underprivileged groups receive dispensation for relevant practical experience if they take on a more advanced study.

Finally, we will conclude that the countries with a clearly developed system of professionalism have invested a great deal in expanding the possibilities for vertical and horizontal mobility within all the professions dealing with young children.

Everywhere in Europe, professionalism in childcare is on the political agenda. The 'care concept' is being increasingly set aside and childcare is becoming imbedded in a larger whole in which the parenting and social functions are being given an important place. Because of this, the professions in the childcare sector are being radically reformed in many European countries. Some countries are choosing a social-pedagogic vision, others have integrated childcare into the educational system.

Within the EU and other international organizations, there is a consensus that the competencies and qualifications of staff members in the professions dealing with young children must be upgraded. There is a fascinating debate going on concerning the manner in which this must be done. The development of action-oriented competencies which give the staff member the ability to deal with complex situations and to develop his/her own practical pedagogic knowledge is a central focus here.

2

The debate on professionalism in Early Childhood Education and Care in Europe

2.1. Equal opportunity policy puts professionalism in Early Childhood Education and Care on the European agenda in the eighties and nineties

2.1.1. European Commission Childcare Network maps out professionalism in childcare

Early Childhood Education and Care lies within the authority of the national states (such as in Luxembourg and The Netherlands) or of the regions, communities or Länder (such as in Germany and Belgium): the European Union has no legal authority over this policy domain. Since the mid-1980s, however, the debate on professionalism has been strongly influenced by the EU (Moss 2003c). The greatest influence from the European Union on the debate concerning professionalism in childcare comes from the European policy on offering women equal opportunities in the labour market. This granting of equal rights between men and women had been included in the Treaty of Rome as early as 1957 (Moss 1991a: 60). In 1982, The European Community launched its 'First Action Programme on the Promotion of Equal Opportunities for Women' (1982-1985) and thus recognised the connection between the expansion of a child-care sector and equal opportunities for women in the labour market (Vandenbroeck, 2004: 210). As a consequence of this First Action Programme, the European Com-mission proceeded with the creation of a 'Childcare Network and other measures to combine work and family'. This Network was composed of experts from each of the twelve Member States, under the chairmanship of Peter Moss, professor at the London Institute of Education (Humblet, in Vandenbroeck, 1991b).

This Childcare Network of the European Commission received a mandate for ten years (from 1986 to 1996) and has had an extremely important influence on how one thinks about the quality of the provisions for children and the professionalism of the staff members in the EU Member States. The Network has undertaken numerous actions on three themes: quality of provisions for young children, parental leave and men as caregivers. (Cohen, 2004). Before the Childcare Network started, the landscape of childcare in Europe had not yet been mapped out. Moreover, there was no consensus as to what good childcare actually was. (Peeters, 2005a: 33). The first report by the Network (Moss, 1988) made, for the first time, a comparative study of childcare and parental leave regulations in the European Union. The differences among the Member States of that time proved to be extremely great, both in the number of subsidized places available and in the professionalism of the staff members. Denmark was, in the EC of the day with twelve Member States, the absolute frontrunner: in this Scandinavian country, there was a place in daycare for nearly half of the children under three years of age. Belgium and France tied for second place with 20% each. Wealthy countries, such as Germany, the Netherlands and the United Kingdom proved to have places available for only 2 to 3% of the children. It was also surprising to observe which major differences there were in the levels of training: Denmark was again the frontrunner with a training course of three and a half years. Belgium scored very poorly with its training course at the level of vocational education. These comparative studies done by the Network on the various levels of training were discussed everywhere in Europe at numerous conferences (Peeters, Braam, Van den Heede, 1991; Moss, 1991a; Peeters, 1992a; Peeters, Vandenbroeck, 1993; Peeters, 1994; Vandenbroeck, 1995). In 1991, the Network published the brochure 'Quality in Services for Young Children, a discussion paper' (Balaguer, Penn, Mestres, 1991). In this document, the authors strove to develop criteria for high quality childcare. The brochure was circulated in the various Member States by the national representatives of the Network, with the intention to start a discussion on these criteria (Moss, 1994: 5-11). For the first time, a frame of reference was created that made it possible for researchers and policy makers to test the situation in their own regions or countries against that of other Member States.

The activities of the Network also had an impact on the policy decisions of the EU: in 1992, the governments of the Member States accepted the recommendations on childcare. These recommendations were more than a call for action, they included a series of concrete principles and objectives concerning the manner in which the Member States could convert these recommendations into practice (Moss, 2004b).

2.1.2. Concrete objectives on professionalism

At the end of its mandate (1995), the Network published a new brochure: 'Quality targets in services for young children. Proposals for a ten-year plan.' In this brochure, the results of the discussions on quality within the Member States were moulded into forty objectives which the Member States would be required to put into practice by the beginning of 2006. This action programme contained interesting objectives in the areas of professionalism in the early years.

In targets 25 and 26, the Network phrased its action programme for 2006 as follows: 'A minimum of 60% of the staff members who, in the collective provisions, work directly with children, must have a bachelor's degree that includes – both in theory and in practice – the education and developmental psychology of the child. All the training courses must be composed of modules. All the staff members in services for young children (both in collective early childhood provisions and in family day carers) who do not have these bachelor's degrees must have access to these training courses that are to be organised on an alternating basis. In this way, it should be possible to obtain the necessary qualifications via various paths and at the course member's own tempo. Alongside of this, all staff members, both family day carers and those working in the collective provisions, have the right to continuous refresher courses or in-service training courses' (Moss, 1995).

In order to take into account the specific situations of the family day carers, the Network argues in favour of setting up a modular training system that would consist of various levels of qualifications, depending upon how many of the modules were completed. According to the Network, the employees with a diploma or certificate at the level of vocational secondary education, such as the Belgian childcare workers and the French *auxiliaires de puériculture*, should be given the chance to obtain the higher qualifications via the modular system. With a system of modules such as this, their work experience would be assessed and taken into account.

By being confronted with the objectives of the European Network, those in the Member States became conscious of the fact that there was still a long road ahead of them. In many countries, a diploma was only required for some areas of childcare and the existing training courses were shorter – in a large number of the Member States – than what the Network feels is necessary.

Objective 29 determined that 20% of the personnel was to consist of men. By the beginning of the new millennium, the gender aspect in the provisions for young children was to be put on the agenda in various Member States (Peeters, 2007).

These Network criteria have not yet lost their sense of urgency and, in 2004, were published once again by the magazine 'Children in Europe' (Moss, Balaguer, 2004). The objectives have, up through the present, remained a source of inspiration for the advocates of upgrading the educational level of the personnel in the provisions for young children in Europe.

2.1.3. The European Social Fund makes funding available for the upgrading of professionalism in the early years

The impact of Europe went further than only policy advice from the Childcare Network. Through the European Social Fund, significant funds were made available to be converted into projects for the training of childcare workers (Moss, 1991a). The European Social Fund (ESF) saw childcare as an important driving force in offering women equal opportunities on the labour market. Starting in the early 1990s, employment and training projects in childcare were set up all over Europe under the auspices of the New Opportunities for Women programme by the ESF. Thanks to the means made available by the ESF for transnational cooperation, these NOW projects from the various Member States could now cooperate with each other on themes concerning professionalism in childcare (NOW The Letters, 1, 2 and 3).

2.2. Increase in aging population demands an increase in the professionalism in the early years

Since the beginning of the new millennium, early childhood education and care has been high on the political agenda of both the international organisations and the nation states (Osgood 2006: 2; Moss, 2006: 30) for the sake of the sharp rise in the aging population in Europe.

Around 2030, the working population in the European Union will revert from the 303 million that it is now to 280 million. In order to absorb the negative effects of this demographic evolution, everyone within the European Union must join the workforce and the birth rate in the EC countries must increase (in 2002, this was just under 1.5 for the EC). Within the framework of the European Employment Strategy (Lisbon Strategy), the ultimate goal is complete employment (European Commission 2005: 27) with an employment rate of 70% as the concrete target for 2010. Luxembourg has an employment rate of 62%, Lithuania 61%, Belgium, at the moment, is stranded at 60% and Italy at 56%.

In all of the Member States in the European Union, the employment of women is still sorely lower than that of men (22% lower). In order to absorb the effects of the aging population, the employment rate for women must be raised (Joint Employment Report 2004/5). The European Commission has as a primary target 60 procent towards 2010 (European Commission, 2005: 5). As far as the employment of women is concerned, the Scandinavian countries, with their strongly developed, high quality network of childcare, are doing very well: Iceland, Norway, Sweden and Denmark are the frontrunners in Europe when it comes to the employment of women (European Commission 2005: 28). The Scandinavian countries, moreover, have succeeded in combining a high rate of female employment with a high birth rate (Esping-Anderson 2002:71).

In order to increase the employment rate among women, measures must be taken – according to the European Union – in the areas of childcare and maternity and parental leave (Moss, 2004:12). As early as 1992, the European Commission made a recommendation to the Member States (92/241/EEC) in which they were requested to takes measures so that men and women could more easily combine the tasks of work and family. Ten years later, at the Barcelona Summit Conference in 2002, the European ministers decided that the objective of complete employment made it essential – towards 2010 – to provide childcare for 90% of the children between 3 and 12 years of age and for at least 33% of the children under three years of age (European Commission, 2005:33).

Early childhood provisions are, therefore, of essential importance for the European Union in order to remain competitive in a global economy.

Early childhood education is, however, also important from the social-economic perspective. According to Esping-Andersen, female employment is the most effective means for combating social exclusion and poverty (Esping-Andersen, 2002:92). In order to achieve this, a woman-friendly policy must be wielded and childcare plays a key role in this. Early childhood provisions are, therefore, an important means of promoting the social inclusion of groups that are in danger of missing the boat within this global capitalism (Dalberg and Moss, 2005). Early childhood education and care increases the employment possibilities for single mothers and parents from underprivileged groups. This makes it possible for underprivileged groups to take part in the active welfare state and, in this way, to climb out of the poverty.

A third reason why childcare is on the political agenda is because provisions for young children also have an educational role to play. If the European economy wants to remain competitive in the future, it must – with a focus on the aging population – ensure that everyone in the future generation (thus, also children from ethnic minorities and under-privileged groups) is well educated in order to be able to fill the expected shortages on the labour market.

Everywhere in Europe, a strong belief prevails that quality early childhood education and care can give young children a good start. In this vein, the British Prime Minister, Gordon Brown, proclaimed the 21st century to be the century of 'Universal childcare and early years services.' The British government was greatly impressed by the results of the lon-gitudinal EPPE study (Sylva, Melhuish, Sammons, Siraj-Blatchford Taggart, 2004): 'The government has started to recognise that investing in good quality early years services is crucial as it lays the foundation for children's effective learning, improves their social, cognitive and emotional development and has a positive impact on their health and edu-cational attainment now and later in life. Good quality childcare and early years services are therefore key for the Government's policy targets on social justice and equality, social and community regeneration and economic growth.' (Day Care Trust, 2004: 16).

In Germany, the demand for quality childcare for all children is on the agenda due to the poor performance in the OECD PISA study of 2001 (Oberhuemer, 2005:11). From the 2004 OECD screening of provisions for young children, it appears, moreover, that there is a consensus in Germany that the quality of the provisions must be improved (OECD, 2004: 50).

According to Urban (2006:54), all over the world, human rights – and the rights of chil-dren – are being used as arguments for the development of a network of provisions for young children. At the moment, there is an on-going inquiry on Germany by the Human Rights Commission of the United Nations. The chairman of the Human Rights Commis-sion, Vernon Munoz, has serious reservations about the policy of the German govern-ment concerning provisions for young children: because Germany does not guarantee all young children access to the provisions, the rights of some of these children would be violated. 'The Education system should, to the extent possible, offer a conductive envi-ronment to help breaking the cycles of poverty and social disadvantages, thus promoting equal chances for all. This is particularly true within the context of the demographic changes in the country and the paradigm shift on immigration. Education should thus be the vector of a full inclusion of disadvantaged groups, such as Roma people and per-sons with disabilities within the education system and the society as a whole' (Urban, 2006:54).

In Ireland, as well, the development of a high-quality childcare sector has been on the political agenda since the publication of the OECD report of 2004. 'Over the coming years, significant energies and funding will need to be invested in the field to create a system in tune with the needs of a full employment economy and with new understandings of how children develop and learn' (Urban, 2006:35-36).

Within the scientific community, there is also a consensus on the fact that quality care during the first years of life has a huge positive effect on the development of children. In the most recent OECD report, Starting Strong II (OECD, 2006), an overview of the studies demonstrating this is provided (Andersson, 1992; French National Survey, 1992; Success for all studies, 2002; The Chicago Child-Parent Centres Study, 2002; The longitudinal New Zealand survey, 1992; The United States National Evaluation of Early Head Start, 2003: Longitudinal British EPPE (1997-2007).

The political interest in early childhood education and care in the 21st century can, therefore, be explained as an economic concern: if Europe wants to maintain its competitive position in the world market, then – because of the decrease in the working population – as many people as possible must join the workforce. Therefore, the birth rate must rise and female employment must increase.

Childcare plays an important role in making the combination of work and family possible. The socially underprivileged groups must also join the workforce and need, therefore, childcare. At the same time, Europe needs well-educated people; early childhood education is seen as a basis for school achievements later on. From the viewpoint of human rights and the rights of children, it is important that all children have the same access to quality provisions: early childhood education and care can, namely, make an important contribution in breaching the circles of poverty and discrimination.

2.2.1. High quality childcare demands well-trained people

In order to create a basis for 'good quality childcare', it is, according to the researchers, necessary 'to create and sustain workforce with the skills and knowledge to deliver universal services of high quality' (Cameron, 2004:4; Mac Naughton, Rolfe et al., 2001; Dali, 2005; Mac Naughton, 2005).

'Aktuelle Forschungsergebnisse weisen deutlich darauf hin, dass die Profession – bzw.

Ihre Entwicklung – Grundlage dafür ist, die politischen Zielen des quantitatieven und qualitatieven Ausbaus der Kinderbetreuung zu realisieren' (Urban, 2005:9).

A document from the British Government states it as follows: 'The early years workforce is critical in giving children the best start in life. A better qualified workforce, and with more workers trained to professional level, plays a crucial role in determining the quality of the provisions' (Department for Education and Skills, 2005: 24-25).

The Organisation of Economic Cooperation and Development (OECD) also shares this view on the importance of a well-trained workforce in early childhood education and care. In a report on the future of women's professions, the OECD stated, as early as 1997, that there was a tendency in most of the industrialized countries to adopt higher qualifications for the health care and childcare professions (OECD, 1997: 167).

In 'Starting Strong I', an overview of Early Childhood Education and Care in industrialized countries, the OECD talks about the 'growing educational and social responsibilities of the early years workforce'. 'Quality early childhood education and care depends on strong staff training and fair working conditions across the sector' (OECD, 2001: 11).

In the most recent report, 'Starting Strong II', the OECD talks about the prevailing consensus concerning the fact that higher educational requirements increase the quality of the provision of services for young children (OECD, 2006: p. 161). 'The evidence is strong that improved training and qualifications levels raise the quality of interaction and pedagogy in ECEC services.' 'Research from many countries supports the view that quality in the early childhood field requires adequate training.' 'Research shows the link between strong training and support of staff and the quality of ECEC services (Bowman et al., 2000; CQCO Study Team, 1995; EC Childcare Network, 1996; Whitebook et al., 1998). 'In particular, staff who have more formal education and more specialised early childhood training provide more stimulating, warm and supportive interactions with children' (CQCO Study Taem; NICHD, 1997; Phillipsen et al. 1997, EPPE, 2004).

Recently, a longitudinal EPPE study[1] in the UK clearly demonstrated that there is a connection between the level of education of the staff of the provisions and the later school results of the children in primary education. It has an enormous effect on children from underprivileged economic environments and on non-native-speaking children (Sylva, 2004).

---

1   The Effective Provision of Pre-school Education project is a British longitudinal study of children between the ages of three and seven that measures the effects of pre-school education on the development of children and that seeks to determine the characteristics of 'effective practice'.

In the conclusion of the EPPE study, it is stated as follows: 'Settings that have staff with higher qualifications, especially with a good proportion of trained teachers (Bachelor level) on the staff, show higher quality and the children make more progress and better social/behavioural gains.' (Sylva, 2004: 56).

The positive effect of higher qualifications was also confirmed by an American study (Peisner-Feinberg, 1997; 2001). In his overview of recent literature on the effect of pre-school programmes, Melhuish (2004:46) also comes to the same conclusion in reference to the development of children from underprivileged milieus: the level of education of the educators whose work involves young children between 0 and 5 years of age is one of the most important factors in stimulating the development of children.

Osgood (2006:5) also confirms this trend: 'There is a widespread support for the potentially beneficial consequences of heightened professionalism for practitioners.'

This theme is also under discussion in Flanders. In 2004, the Board of Directors of Kind en Gezin [Child and Family, the governmental organisation] decided that: 'Training courses and competency acquisition are exceedingly important for the general quality and for all forms of childcare. For that reason, the competency levels of the childcare staff members should be raised' (RVB/2004/0526/DOC. 151).

2.2.2. Large differences in professionalism among the various countries

Peter Moss, the former chairman of the Childcare Network of the European Commission, sees, however, a contrast between, on the one hand, the discourse by governments which demands more professionalism in the childcare professions and, on the other hand, the reality in numerous European countries: 'In many countries the present workforce is problematic, being not only undesirable but probably unsustainable too, and requires change' (Moss, 2006:31).

Urban also supports Moss in this: 'Die unterprofessionalisierung vor allem des 'Childcare sectors' steht in krassem Gegensatz zu den wachsenden Anforderungen an ihre Arbeit. Die Komplexität wächst vor allem durch die zunehmende Diversität bei Kinder und Familien in allen modernen Gesellschaften' (Urban, 2006:8).

This is also the case for Flanders. In the 'Starting Strong II' report, the OECD repeats its concern about the low educational level of the childcare workers in Flanders (OECD, 2006: 293).

Moreover, Flanders has not followed the trend to organise a training course at the Bachelor level (OECD, 1997). The training course in Childcare (seventh year of a vocational training course) that has been in fashion since 1997, is one that remains within the vocational educational system.

Cameron and Moss, the coordinators of a large research project on Care work in Europe, are adding another aspect to the need for a higher professionalisation of the jobs in childcare. 'The European Union sees the care work not only as a precondition of employment but also as a source of that employment.' But at the same time as wanting more jobs, the EU has emphasized the importance of these jobs being of 'good quality'. Quality of employment is central to the EU's objective of becoming a knowledge-based economy (European Commission, 2001) and, within a short time, quality of work has become major subject of discussion, one which has been at the top of the European political agenda since the Lisbon summit. Otherwise, the argument runs, an expansion of employment might simply produce more poor quality jobs, with detrimental consequences for employees and society alike (Esping-Andersen, et al., 2001). Rather than seeing a choice needing to be made, the EC is clear that Europe 'needs to address both the quantity and the quality of jobs' (Cameron, Moss, 2007: 4).

2.2.3. Conclusion

The European Union, the OECD and the individual European Member States all argue that it is essential – for demographic-economic, social-economic and educational reasons – to offer childcare to everyone in the future (Universal ECEC). The great importance that the political world attaches to the development of the provisions for young children offers interesting perspectives for launching new ideas in the future. In Flanders, the social function of childcare and of the ECE-schools (*kleuterschool*) is on the political agenda of the Ministers of Welfare and of Education (Vervotte, 2007; Vandenbroeck, 2007) and, in the United Kingdom, this has made the development of Children's Centres possible. At the same time, however, this political interest contains an element of risk. The government can find a way to exert more supervision over the families and the children in order to realise previously determined outcomes that are based on a so-called non-normative and universal knowledge. Such an approach ignores the social-economic context in which child-rearing (upbringing) takes place and offers little space for important values which must provide direction for the activities in the services for young children.

'We are confronted by an increasingly dominant discourse that offers a depressing and alienating view, in which rhetoric of choice and diversity masks an actuality of control and uniformity; that stifles difference, experimentation and democracy by insisting on there being one objective and scientifically-determined truth, both about outcomes and methods; and that reduces children and adults to the position of units of human capital' (Dahlberg en Moss: 2007: 11).

At the same time, it has been established that there is also a growing consensus within Europe in favour of increasing the quality of the employment of childcare workers. There is, however, no consensus on the way in which the upgrading of professionalism should occur. 'Die Frage, wie das Profil der 'Early childhood profession' in Zukunft aussehen wird, bestimmt zunehmend die Europäische Reformdebatte. Eine einheitliche Konzeptualisierung der frühkindlichen Profession ist bislang nicht erkennbar; ein Konsens über die fachliche rolle der Menschen, die in der Betreuung – und Bildungsinstitutionen tätig sind, besteht in Europa nicht' (Urban, 2006:9).

Therefore, most of the Member States must reflect seriously on the type of professionalism that they are striving for.

It is, therefore, necessary to describe the concept of professionalism in more precise terms and to work out what kind of professionalism is required in childcare.

3

What kind of professionalism do we need?

3.1. Professionalism: *un mot flou*

The term professionalism is often used in the sense of a general upgrading of the professional qualifications, an improvement in the work situation and an upgrading of the status of the profession. In a stricter – more sociological – definition, one talks about the three dimensions of professionalism: 'Unique body of knowledge, restrictive entry and protected identity' (Crompton, 1987). Other authors add a set of well-defined professional ethics to this, within which, among other things, the assumption of a detached attitude towards the client is seen as essential (Noddings, 1986; Moyles, 2001; Osgood, 2006; Moss, 2006).

Various social groups may, however, have completely different ideas as to what precisely constitutes the professionalism of a profession.

According to Hoyle (1969) (quoted in Aelterman, 1995:200), the concepts of professionalism, profession and professional have, in particular, symbolic and evaluative connotations. The various actors within the sector (employers, policy makers, trade unions, parents…) will have a different interpretation of this ideal image of the profession of childcare educator. In this respect, Bourdoncle (1995: 144) made the following differentiation between: *une professionalité réquise, une professionalité révendiquée et une professionalité reconnue.*

Translated to childcare, we can, on the one hand, talk about a professionalism that is required from the government (*professionalité réquise*) which refers to the diploma requirements in the daycare centres. On the other hand, the professionalism that is demanded by some of the family day carers (*professionalité révendiquée*) in many countries is, however, something else entirely; they want better working conditions and an employee's contract. The third form of professionalism (*professionalité reconnue*) refers to the recognition and appreciation by the government and the public. When we think, for example, about the various degrees of recognition/appreciation that are given to kindergarten teachers and the childcare workers, it is clear that the professionalism of the childcare worker is much less appreciated and valued than that of the kindergarten teachers.

Bourdoncle therefore calls *professionalité*: *un mot flou et une notion ambiguë*. Kaddouri (2005 : 145) talks about '*Le Clair obscur de la professionalisation*'. '*Sa polysémie, amplifiée par son usage indifférencié, laisse subsister des confusions et des ambiguïtés qui risquent de cacher les fonctions et les rôles des dispositifs et des pratiques qu'il désigne.*' Kaddouri points out that this is the greatest danger for professions '*qui ne disposent pas de modèle achevée dans la matière*'. Professions in the childcare sector do not possess a clear concept of professionalism and are, consequently, extremely sensitive to the ambiguity which Kaddouri warns about.

It is, therefore, not surprising that there are a great many different notions of professionalism in childcare and that the various actors in the childcare sectors maintain different views on how this professionalism is to be defined.

The similarity with that other, widely used, concept, 'quality,' is, therefore, striking (Dahlberg, Moss and Pence, 1999), (Pirard, 2005:60). It is therefore necessary to give the concept of professionalism a more adequate interpretation.

3.2. Functional sociological visions on professionalism

'In its narrow, more sociological definition, professionalism is about defining and defending borders through a specific knowledge base, knowledge monopoly, long academic education and control over who may practice, and over occupational ethics' (Moss, 2006: 38).

Sorel and Wittorski recently compiled an overview of the definitions of both 'occupation' (*métier*) and 'profession' (*profession*). Occupation refers to an activity in which 'manual,' and 'craftsmanship' are the dominant characteristics while a 'profession', is characterized by the intellectual or rational and the social significance of the activity plays a more central role.

Sorel and Wittorski, in turn, take on the French literature and we also find comparable definitions in Bourdoncle (1991), Abella (1992) and Jobert (1985) of what constitutes a 'profession'. Freidson (1984) takes it the furthest in his differentiation between occupation and 'profession':

1. 'la profession définit ses propres normes d'étude et de formation

2. la pratique professionnelle reçoit souvent sa reconnaissance légale sous la forme d'un permis d'exercer

3. les instances d'admission et d'habilitation sont composées par des membres de la profession

4. la législation relative à la profession est en majeur partie l'œuvre de la profession elle-même

5. le praticien est relativement indépendant du jugement et du contrôle des profanes'.

Mioche (2005) has compiled an overview of the Anglo-Saxon sociology literature (Durkheim, Weber, the sociology of interaction) on professionalism and she also arrives at the five criteria of professionalism.

With respect to the occupations dealing with young children, the debate on 'profession' and 'professionalism in the early years' has also been going on for some time, according to Urban (2005: 2). Various authors have made an attempt to describe what it is that must be understood when talking about professionalism in the professions dealing with young children (professionalism in the early years). Vandenbroeck used a similar description – first for the family day carer (1991: 157) and later for the staff member at out-of-school childcare facilities (1993:127) – of how the professional childcare worker differs from the amateur. According to him, there are five traditional criteria that determine whether or not a certain social practice is professionalized:

1. There must be a formal recognition of the profession. In other words, there must be an official, generally accepted manner in which to differentiate between who practices this profession and who does not.

2. Moreover, the access to the profession must be regulated. Diplomas, certificates and/or selection criteria must limit the access to the profession and, at the same time, guarantee professional competence.

3. There must be a common deontology; that is, generally accepted regulations on the manner in which the profession is to be practiced.

4. Also, the collective use of the same technical language (jargon) is an important condition for professionalism.

5. Finally, professionalism demands that the professional group can act autonomously. This means that it has its own responsibilities that cannot be assumed by others.

3.3. Technical concepts of professionalism and childcare: a difficult marriage

The manner in which professionalism is interpreted in professions with young children does not, according to a number of authors, agree with these functionalistic sociological definitions of professionalism. Here, we will examine a number of the bottlenecks more closely.

3.3.1. Professionalism and emotional involvement

One traditionally accepted condition that determines whether or not a social practice is also accepted as a profession is that a professional relationship exists between the professional and the client. In the professions of medicine and law, this presumes that the professional maintains a certain distance and does not become too personally involved with his/her client. In a study on professionalism in the early years, Calder (2005:1) indicates that this interpretation of distance is undesirable. For the welfare professions, as well, a distance with respect to the client has certainly been observed (Kunneman, 2005a), (Roggen, 2004). According to Janet Moyles (2001:81), someone who works with young children must not be distant but must, on the contrary, be emotionally involved with the child.

'It seems impossible to work effectively with very young children without the deep and sound commitment signified by the use of words like 'passionate'. Yet this very symbolisation gives a particular emotional slant to the work of early childhood practitioners which can work against them in their everyday roles and practices, bringing into question what constitutes professionalism and what being a 'teacher' means.'

Various authors (Hochschild,1983; Price, 2001; Colley, 2006), have pointed out the importance of being able to manage emotions when dealing with children. In connection with this, they talk about: 'Emotional labour, such work entails learning to manage one's own feelings in order to evoke particular feelings in other people.' (Hochschild, 1983:6-7). Coley (2006) also emphasises the importance of managing one's feelings when working in childcare.

Bosse-Platiére, Dehier, Fleury and Loutre (1995:51) describe the deeply rooted objections against the traditional conditions of emotional detachment as follows: 'Un monde éducatif professionnel n'entraîne-t-il pas une certaine déshumanisation?' Professionalism assumes, according to the more traditional definitions, a certain distance, a non-personal involvement of the professional with respect to the person upon whom the profession has bearing. This aspect elicits a great deal of resistance among parents and many others. The raising of young children presumes, after all, extremely great emotional involvement. Noddings (1986) has extensively documented this position from a feministic perspective. She is a fervent opponent of institutionalising and professionalizing the care professions. Canella (1997: 167) does not agree with Noddings' objections to professionalisation, but warns us: 'Professionalism in childcare is a dangerous journey.' According to her and to Osgood (2006), professionalisation can be used as a means of garnering power over the private domain and can be a means of governmental control in order to force the care providers into a straightjacket: 'to adopt commercial approaches to the management of provision. ... In neo-liberal discourses there is little room for emotionality or such feminine characteristics that are seemingly unquantifiable or auditable... and emotions are vitally essential to providing good quality provisions to young children.' (Osgood, 2006b:5)

Dalli advocates integrating the concepts of 'love and care' into a new construct of professionalism. She acknowledges the questionable definitions of these concepts but, at the same time, research demonstrates that 'Early Childhood staff report' 'love of children' 'as a strong motivation in their work' (Dalli, 2006a: 9). She sees possibilities in a 'revised notion of love and care', on both the political and pedagogical levels. According to Pierre Boudrieu, the professional 'habitus'[2] of Early Childhood Education can change. By providing this 'love and care' with a different interpretation, the status quo, which prevents the sector from developing a professional status, could be breached. At the same time, an important aspect in working with young children that, thus far, has hardly – or not at all – been given a chance, could then come to the forefront. On the pedagogic level, this would have the advantage that 'caring competency' would no longer be seen as a personality characteristic. 'A care-centred orientation is a relation, something you consciously do from the unending obligation to meet the other as one-caring, then this can be seen as a pedagogical strategy that can be described and observed and thus also taught in teacher education programmes' (Dalli, 2006: 10).

---

2   Habitus, a system of dispositions acquired through a relationship to a certain 'field'. (Dalli, 2006:10)
    Bourdieu describes this concept as follows: 'L'habitus, c'est ce qui nous pousse à nous comporter ainsi que nous nous comportons'. http://www.dialogus2.org/BOU/habitus.html

3.3.2. The professional expert and the 'inexperienced' parent

Bosse-Platière, Dehier, Fleury and Loutre (1995: 51) point to another area of tension: *'Le professionnalisme, n'entraîne-t-il pas aussi une certaine hièrarchisation entre parents et professionnels, entre savoir maternels et savoir acquis, plus professionnalisés, avec une déresponsabilisation des familles?'* More professionalism can strengthen unequal social relationships. There are, after all, two roles that originate from this: that of the expert – in this case, the early childhood worker – and that of the layman, the parent.

Traditional professionalism makes a clear differentiation between the professional and the layman. Moss also points to the danger of expert thinking that is mired in more traditional definitions of professionalism: 'Professionalism is about defining and defending borders through a specific scientific knowledge base, knowledge monopoly, long academic education and control over who may practice, and over occupational ethics. On these counts, the worker as technician might be included within professionalism: indeed, it may increasingly be that 'professionals' are technicians, especially if the professional value of autonomy is subordinated to the increasing regulation of managerial regimes' (Moss, 2006:38).

This type of expert-technician tutor can, for example, translate the final attainment levels, recorded in a detailed educational policy plan, into practice, or can let himself be guided by procedures that are set down in an quality handbook. The expert-technician claims, according to Moss, that his knowledge, practice and objectives are universally applicable and correct.

Moss (2003, 2006) and Cameron (2004) argue for a different vision of the profession: tutors in ECEC must be 'reflective practitioners' who must constantly question their daily child-rearing practices and must, themselves, go in search of new interpretations of the manner in which they relate to children. 'The individual calls upon the thought processes that allows him to identify, interpret, anticipate and decide upon pertinent knowledge' (Aelterman, 1995: 246). The tutor is a kind of researcher, one who reflects and who – just like the children with whom he works – is continually learning and developing, together with them, a practical pedagogical knowledge. The Swedisch researcher Gunilla Dahlberg phrased it as follows:

'The view of the child as co-constructor implies a view of the teacher as co-constructor of culture and knowledge. This view means a twofold professional responsibility, which partly is about dialogue and communicative action with the child, the group of children and the colleagues, partly a reflecting and researching attitude in which the starting point is the work and learning process of both children and the teacher' (In Moss, 2003c: 13).

The expert-technician wants to teach parents how children should be, what their needs are and how parents should fulfil these needs so that the children will develop properly. The teacher-researcher is, however, able to 'create an educational practice together with the children, the parents and the local community' (Vandenbroeck, 1999). Cameron (2004:11) does not advocate an expert-technician, either, but wants a completely different type of ECEC worker. Referring to the Italian pedagogue Malaguzzi (Rinaldi, 2005), she advocates 'a workforce for a rich and competent child'. This teacher-researcher wants – together with the parents – to garner insight into the learning process and the abilities of children, which leads to 'a reversal towards radical reciprocity in the relationship between teacher and parent-child' (Vandenbroeck, 1999).

3.3.3. (Too) many roads lead to professionalism in childcare

One important criterion for professionalism is the regulation of the access to the profession and the manner in which the knowledge and competencies are taught to new professionals. There has been a major change in this area over the past thirty years. Until the early 1980s, professionalism was equated with the implementation of better and longer training. Professionalism was to be realized by limiting access to the profession and guaranteeing professional competence via diplomas and certificates that were issued by schools. Katz (1985) and many of her peers, argued that the professions dealing with young children needed good basic training courses. Also, during the 1980s, experiments were set up in most of the European countries to attempt to increase the professional competence via interactive training, mentoring and theme-oriented refresher courses.

Starting in the 1990s, we see that the discussion on professionalism has been becoming broader: training courses that are organised by schools are not the only way to earn the necessary professional competency as a teacher or childcare worker. Various authors, such as Griffin (1991), Peeters (1993a), Brants (1994), Joos (1994), Quintin (1996), Sciama and Van Turtelboom (1996), Paul (2004), Keersmaekers (2005), and Pirard (2005) have since been able to show that, alongside of training courses offered by schools, refresher courses, short starter training courses, coaching on the work floor and the recognition of earlier acquired competencies can further the expansion of professionalism in the early years. All of these ways of enhancing professional competency contribute to the increase in status of the profession and, in this way, strengthen the professionalism.

Since the 1990s, we see that, under the incentive of European employment initiatives, numerous initial courses are organised that are specifically geared toward practice and which prepare for a few, specific 'new' jobs ('fragmented jobs') in childcare that are based on a technical interpretation of professionalism.

In 1997, the OECD stated that an intensive discussion was going on in many countries concerning the necessity to combine qualified personnel with a greater accessibility for low qualified personnel and, at the same time, to create new, low-cost care centres (OECD, 1997: 188). The OECD researchers asked themselves if the necessary professionalism in the early years is an achievable goal due to the massive influx of low-qualified personnel. According to them, this was only possible if the institutions in which the low qualified personnel end up are not commercial (cooperative or public provisions) and if the government – together with these provisions – develops a consistent approach for training this target group (OECD, 1997:199).

Towards the end of the 1990s, the ideas about competency that had already been strongly developed in the United Kingdom (Durrance, 2007), found their way to the European continent via programmes of the European Social Fund (SERV, 2001, 2005). Official organs lay down the required competencies in professional profiles and endeavor to encourage professionalism by encouraging competencies (Keersmaekers, 2005; Cache, 2007).

In summary, we can argue that, in the mid-1980s, the diploma, as the sole criteria of professionalism, was disbanded and that mentoring and in-service training were implemented. In the 1990s, all kinds of alternative paths began to lead to jobs in childcare. This provides adults who did not have the initial training in their youth with access to a profession in childcare. In a number of European countries, there are, at the moment, many different paths leading to a career in childcare. Various authors, therefore, have been warning that, because of the lack of a clear policy, access to the profession provides insufficient guarantee that the candidates have effectively achieved the necessary competencies. For that reason, they urge the governments to develop a coherent policy that would regulate the access for all professions in childcare, taking into account the high standards that must be set for childcare workers. (Moss, 2006; Cameron, 2004; Peeters, 2006). The OECD also shares this view; they argue in favour of allowing low qualified personnel access to jobs in the care professions while, at the same time, wielding a coherent policy to make the jobs in the care sector more attractive by investing a great deal in training and education, raising the wages and improving the working conditions. (OECD, 1997:202).

3.3.4. The significance of the training course is questioned due to the non-conformity of the technical concept

With the exception of the Scandinavian countries, we have found that, in nearly all industrialised countries, there are movements that object to specific forms of professionalization of the childcare sector (Moss, 2003a; Peeters, 2005a). Regularly, the opponents of professionalization are presented in the popular media. They think in terms of an aloof form of professionalism, as existed in the daycare centres up until the 1970s, that is said to be dangerous for the development of the child. (VTM, 2002, 2006; VRT, 2006). The mother is the best parent for her young child and a childcare worker must, therefore, support the role of the mother as much as possible. It is taken for granted that women have a natural capacity to care for children. The French Minister of Health and Family, Michèle Barzach, put forth the following in 1987: 'On est déformé par la formation. Je ne pense pas qu'il soit nécessaire d' avoir un brevet d'éducation pour élever un enfant. Il a besoin d'amour et de sécurité… Quant à l'amour, les femmes qui choisissent de s'occuper d'enfants le font parce qu' elles les aiment. Sinon, elles feraient autre chose' (in Verba, 2006 : 82).

Cameron, Moss and Owen (1999) have extensively documented this position: women are natural mothers, that is why women are also naturally suited for the profession of childcare worker. They need little training and, because they have only low qualifications, it is normal that they also have a low salary. Childcare is seen – in some European countries by some policy makers and public opinion – as a substitution for the mother, rather than a fully-fledged job for which you need to be trained.

There is also still an extremely strong 'mother-view' within the childcare sector in Flanders that feels that this professionalization is not necessary. Over the past decades, we have seen a spectacular expansion of childcare in the types of childcare that return to the 'ersatz mother image': (family day carer, mini-crèches), while the subsidised daycare centres that are run by professional childcare workers have only moderately profited from the increase in places for children (Vandenbroeck, 2004).

Starting in the 1980s, unemployment has become an important subject on the political agenda. Since the early 1990s, numerous employment initiatives have been started in Europe to help unschooled or low qualified women get jobs in childcare (Vandenbroeck, 1993). These employment initiatives are resistant to an enforced professionalization because that would cut off the access to the childcare professions for underprivileged groups because they do not have a diploma. These initiatives also appeal to the 'mother-model' and do not, therefore, see the use of lengthy training courses. The defendants of this viewpoint can be found among organisations, politicians and labour unions which are dedicated to finding employment for long-term unemployed and low qualified women. Vandenbroeck (2004: 205) has demonstrated how this has also had an impact on expansion of childcare. Politicians, labour unions and employment organisations see childcare as one of the few employment opportunities for this group of unqualified women (Peeters, 1993b:16).

A former Flemish Minister of Education put it as follows: 'If we continue to drive up the diploma requirements for a number of occupations, this can lead to a dual society in which the non-qualified or low-qualified population do not get any chances.' (Vandenbossche, 1994). The inclination against professionalization was – and still is – extremely strong in most Member States with the exception of the Scandinavian countries. Because of this, there are no diploma requirements for new sections of the childcare sector (Peeters, 2005:52; Vandenbroeck, 2005:23). 'In care work, as household services or in social care, the distinction between paid and unpaid work dissolves: the work is the same, the gender of the doer the same, all that changes is the relationship of the doer to the labour market.' (Cameron, Moss, 2007: 11).

Professionalization of the early years professions is, in other words, still the subject of intense debate.

3.4. Working towards a normative, evolutionary and participatory concept of professionalism oriented on quality of action

3.4.1. Plea for normative professionalism in education and welfare

Aelterman (1995:237) advocates a new concept of professionalism that takes into account the normative sphere which is incorporated in training and practice. Kunneman (2005b:268) shares that opinion for occupations in the welfare sector. According to him, a purely technically-oriented professionalism ignores all the value-bound elements of professional actions. In welfare work – and, therefore, also in childcare – he argues, therefore, for a normative professionalism. Acting professional is, according to Kunneman, bound to existential and moral sources of orientation: personal involvement, attention, integrity, loyal cooperation with colleagues and a sense of social responsibility, as well as creativity, curiosity and an innovative ability. Interesting in this connection is the work of Trijntje Roggen (2004:153-159) who, in a PhD thesis, put this normative professionalism into practice for the children with special needs sector in a 'normative protocol for critical reflection.'

3.4.2. Professionalism in a developmental perspective

As early as 1995, Aelterman (1995:242) advocated a concept of professionalism that was based on a developmental perspective. In connection with this, she cited Kremer-Hanyon (1991: 81): 'Occupations go through a dynamic process of professionalization, in which dilemma, doubts, lack of stability and divergence become integral aspects of profession.'
The *Centre de la Recherche sur la Formation* from Paris, led by Jean-Marie Barbier has set up numerous studies concerning professionalization that are based on a dynamic perspective of professionalism. The researchers of the CRF have reached a more workable definition of professionalism. Barbier (2005:126) argues that the notion of professionalization is used differently today:
'*La professionalisation apparue d'abord dans la sociologie des professions, notamment américaine, pour désigner le processus de naissance et de structuration de groupes organisés, autonomes, et défendant leurs intérêts, notamment en contrôlant l'accès à la profession et à son exercice, cette notion est aujourd'hui de plus en plus utilisée en Europe, et dans*

l'univers de la gestion et de la formation pour désigner le développement de différentes actions et initiatives référées à une intention d'élaboration et d'actualisation de compétences.'

For Barbier, professionalization is *'l'organisation sociale d'un espace de développement de compétences dans un contexte d'activité évolutive.'*

Professionalization is a process whose objective it is to create new competencies which, in turn, must improve and accommodate the activities. Professionalization refers to the process of the improvement and the development of competencies, such that the quality of the work is related to the expertise of the individual.

3.4.3. Professionalism and participation of the staff members

According to Sorel and Wittorski (2005:247), there is professionalization of the individual, of the (professional) activities and of the organizations. The professionalization of the individual has to do with the development of knowledge, skills and competencies and with the expansion of a self-image and of the place of the individual in the professional world. Professionalization of the individual *'relève d'une construction identitaire 'pour soi,' les savoirs et les compétences développés servant en quelque sorte de 'marqueur identitaire'.'*

Professionalization of the activities refers to *'la formalisation de référentiels 'préscrits ou réels' que l'on pourrait assimiler à des bornes de territorialité ou des systèmes de justification à destination de l'espace des professions, qui remplissent des fonctions identitaires 'pour autrui'.'*

The professionalization of the organizations is *'construire les repères d'exercice du métier, repères qui serviront tout autant à l' interne pour organiser les activités, qu' à l'externe pour communiquer l'expertise de l'organisation.'*

For this study, it is important to know how individuals develop their professionalism. According to Sorel and Wittorski (2005:251), it is essential that the individual who is 'professionalizing' himself is not reduced to the role of a 'consumer' of the knowledge that is dished up to him. The individual who is the subject of a process of professionalization is, according to Sorel and Wittorski, a co-constructor of knowledge; he must, during the training, be part of the knowledge development under the supervision of the trainer.

The researchers at the Centre de la Recherche sur la Formation in Paris, do not assume that professionalism is something static that is acquired and must be protected by regulating the access, but see it, rather, as a process within which individuals, activities and organisations are continually in evolution and, together, aim at change. At the same time, the researchers at the CRF assume that the individuals make a major contribution to this process of professionalization; they are co-authors or co-constructors of that evolving professionalism.

3.4.4. The creation of 'quality of action' within complex relationships with colleagues, parents and neighborhood

Here, the French authors find a connection with a number of their British colleagues. As Osgood puts it: 'A professional identity is performatively constituted; being professional is a performance, which is about what practitioners do at particular times rather than a universal indication of who they are' (Osgood, 2006:12).
Maning-Morton also emphasizes the importance of what staff members do in practice for the understanding of what professionalism is all about: 'Professionalism in the early years must be understood in terms of the day-to-day details of practitioners' relationships with children, parents, and colleagues; relationships that demand high levels of physical, emotional and personal knowledge and skill' (Manning-Morton, 2006: 42).

Dalli sums up, in one sentence, the core of the discussion on professionalism: 'In the early childhood sector we are making a new profession' (Dalli, 2003:11). According to Dalli, the sector is in need of a description of professionalism that falls back on existing definitions but, at the same time, also answers to the specific context and the day-to-day reality of Early Childhood Education. 'This reality is complex; work in early childhood education requires brain as well as heart; knowledge as well as care and love; action as well as reflection; skill as well as clarity; it requires humour and perhaps also a touch of madness.' (Dalli, 2003:11).

Oberhuemer argues that professionalism is a vague and disputed concept but, nonetheless, there is, according to her, a consensus on the fact that 'Professionalism is linked to "quality of action" within a specific occupational field' (Oberhuemer, 2000:4). Oberhuemer advocates democratic professionalism. 'Democratic professionalism is a concept based on participatory relationships and alliances. It foregrounds collaborative, co-operative action between professional colleagues and other stakeholders. It emphasises engaging and networking with the local community.' (Oberhuemer, 2005:13). Oberhuemer describes four levels of action: interaction with children, the management and leadership of the centre, the partnership with the parents and professional knowledge that is based on: 'Multiple ways of knowing, an understanding that knowledge is in fact contestable… It implicates the professional skill to sensitively discuss pedagogical and ethical viewpoints against a background of increasing cultural, social and economic diversity, to recognize and examine both personal and publicly-endorsed assumptions' (Oberhuemer, 2005: 14).

3.5. Conclusion

There is a growing consensus within Europe on the necessity of upgrading professionalism in the childcare sector. There is, however, no agreement on the way in which this upgrading must occur. It is, therefore, necessary to better define the concept of professionalism in the professions dealing with young children. Traditional sociological definitions of professionalism are difficult to apply to professions in the childcare sector. Childcare is in need of a professionalism in which the use of emotions is given an important place in the work with children and their parents. For that reason, there is a tendency to head in the direction of a normative professionalism in which there is a place for personal involvement, attention, sense of responsibility, creativity, curiosity and innovative ability. A concept of professionalism in early childhood education and care, therefore, is not based on the concept of a technical expert: the knowledge, skills and competencies that are required in early childhood education, after all, are not universally applicable. We need a type of professionalism that assumes that teachers must be 'reflective practitioners' or teacher-researchers who must continually question their pedagogical practices and, together with the parents and the children, must create an educational practice that is being constantly renewed and improved.

By the process of professionalization, we mean the development of various actions and initiatives whose intention it is to develop and realize competencies. In order to professionalize the staff members, it is essential that the individual himself makes a major contribution to this process; he/she must be a co-constructor of this continually evolving professionalism. The professionalization of individuals is a learning process in which, again and again, meaning is given to the interpretation of the profession and this is continually done in relationship to others: the colleagues, the parents and the children.

In light of this, the professionalization process can be seen as a social practice that is the consequence of interaction between, on the one hand, social evolutions, policy measures and new scientific insights and, on the other hand, the researchers, the staff at childcare centres and the users, the parents and the children.

In connecting with this, Bourdieu talks about *'une construction sociale, le produit de tout un travail social de construction d'un groupe et d'une* représentation *de ce groupe qui s'est glissé en douce dans la science du monde social'* (Bourdieu, 1992: 212-213).

4

Professionalism and gender in the professions for young children

4.1. The connection between professionalism and gender in ECEC professions

Cameron has studied the relationship between the professionalization of the childcare professions and the participation of the male staff members (Cameron, 2006). She found that, in most European countries, there was a tendency towards increased professionalization: 'In England this shift is taking place both at the policy level, with the aim of addressing goals such as improving the social and educational outcomes for children and increasing the availability and accessibility of early childhood services, and at the sector level, with increased identification with the notion of being a 'professional' (Cameron, 2006: 69). In some countries, the tendency towards professionalization has become even clearer due to the development of a model of professionalism in which there is one type of staff member who is highly qualified (bachelor's or master's degree). This is the case in Denmark, Sweden and New Zealand for all facilities for children between the ages of 0 and 5 (Moss, 2004) and in Belgium for kindergarten (2.5-5-year olds). Cameron states that, in these countries, 'professionalization in terms of extensive training, a unique body of knowledge and a distinctive occupational identity was achieved with an almost entirely female workforce, and before efforts were made to recruit more men' (Cameron, 2006: 71). A high degree of professionalism does not apparently automatically lead to an increase in the number of male staff members. 'A process of professionalization is not necessarily related to increased numbers of men working in early childhood services: both processes can clearly occur independently of one another' (Cameron, 2006: 76). One example of this is New Zealand where, by 2012, all staff members who work with children from 0 to 6 years old must have a bachelor's degree and where only 1% of the teachers are men (Farquhar, 2006).

However, we have also seen that there are countries where it appears to be possible to attract more men, without there being a high degree of professionalization. In Scotland, where 40% of the childcare workers have not achieved level 2 (Miller, 2006: 3), excellent results have, nonetheless, been achieved in attracting male staff members. The 'Men in Childcare' project in Scotland has succeeded in motivating 900 men to take some form of – generally low-school – training (Spence, 2007).

But then again, there is certainly a relationship between the professionalism of the childcare professions and the attractiveness of these professions for men. Men will only be attracted to jobs in the childcare sector if these jobs emanate a professionalism that is not gender-bound, in other words, that is not based on the maternal role (Peeters, 2005; Cameron, Moss, Owen, 1999). Cameron (2006: 76) states – based on her research with male staff members (Cameron, Moss, Owen, 1999) – that professionalism that is based on 'mother-like practice', is an impediment for the entry of male staff in childcare. In connection with this, Cameron talks about 'dislodging the gendered model of the profession' (Cameron, 2006: 76).

We must redefine the professional identity and the status of the childcare professions. A study of the gender aspects in the professions dealing with young children could contribute to the 'democratic professionalism' as was defined by Oberhuemer: 'Democratic professionalism presupposes an awareness of multiple ways of knowing, an understanding that knowledge is in fact contestable. It requires a willingness and ability to reflect on one's own taken-for-granted beliefs' (Oberhuemer, 2005: 14). In Cameron's opinion, the experiences of male staff members may be able to broaden the collective knowledge base of the profession. By continually questioning the gender-specific aspects in the tradition of the reflective practitioner (Schön, 1983), a new interpretation can be given to the practice of the childcare professions.

Although professionalism in the childcare professions and the entry of men into the profession are not necessarily linked with each other, the type of professionalism is certainly important: a gender-specific interpretation of professionalism will certainly curb the entry of men, while a gender-neutral structure of professionalism will promote it. In the following chapter, we will analyse the evolution of the thinking about a gender-neutral professionalism, and we will underpin the proposition that a gender-neutral interpretation is essential in order to make the childcare sector better disposed towards men.

4.2. The influence of the Childcare Network of the European Commission on the gender theme in ECEC

As previously described, in 1982, the European Union started the first 'Gender Equality Program' with the intention of offering women equal chances in the labour market. Within this framework, in 1986, the Childcare Network of the European Commission was established under the chairmanship of Prof. Peter Moss of London University.

One of the three action items of this Network was the theme 'Men as caregivers'. From a gender-equality perspective, men should take on more tasks within the family and should become more involved in the parenting of young children.

The theme 'Men as caregivers' also came up in the 'Recommendations on Childcare' of the Council of Ministers of the EU (1992): 'Member States commit themselves to promote and encourage, with due respect for freedom of the individual, increased participation by men' (article 6).

In 1993, the Childcare Network invited experts from various European Member States to Ravenna in order to take part in a debate on men as caregivers. The experts agreed that the measures to involve more men in the parenting of their young children would have little effect unless a greater number of male caregivers were employed in the childcare sector (EC Childcare Network, 1993). Male staff members could serve as role models for young fathers and, at the same time, services for young children could play an important part in the development of a new care culture for young children: a culture in which there is also a place for men. Another important argument for employing more men in the provisions for young children was the fact that children would then be confronted with male role models. The Network assumed that this would have an effect on future generations, who would then be more inclined to divide the household and parenting tasks more equally among men and women.

The experts found, however, that, within the EU, there were only a limited number of centres where male staff members formed a significant percentage of the personnel. In most of the European countries, the men made up no more than 1 to 3% of the employees. The Childcare Network, therefore, decided that serious efforts should be made to increase the number of men in the provisions for young children.

In the Scandinavian countries in the early 1990s, various initiatives were taken and campaigns were launched in order to increase the number of male staff members in services for young children (0 to 6 years old). In Denmark, the theme was put on the political agenda in the early 1990s and good results were achieved: 5% male staff members in childcare centres (0 to 3 years old), 9% for the age group 3 to 6 years old and in the mixed age groups (1 to 12 years old) and 25% in out-of-school care.

The Sheffield Children's Centre in the UK has had an equal number of male and female caregivers since the 1980s. (Meleady, Broadhead, 2002) and the Pen Green Family Centre also had nearly as many men as women employed there. At the beginning of the 1990s, a new kind of professionalism was established in these two centres, such that since then, the gender differences have been openly discussed and a gender-neutral interpretation of professionalism has been constructed (Cameron, Moss, Owen, 1999; Meleady, Broadhead, 2002). Childcare workers from both of these centres, researchers and policy makers from Emilia Romagna, (Italy), Norway, Sweden and Denmark formed a group of pioneers who worked closely with the Childcare Network (Jensen, 1998: 128).

Meanwhile, the Network had published the discussion document 'Quality in Services for Young Children' that was translated into all the languages of the EU-12. The theme of male childcare workers was one of the topics in this brochure, about which a discussion was started among researchers, policy makers and representatives of childcare workers within the Member States.

In 1995, the Childcare Network of the European Commission published a report 'Forty Quality Targets in services for young children' in which the discussions that had been carried out within the EU-12 were summarized into 40 objectives for quality that the Member States would have to achieve within the following 10 years. Objective 29 of this document states that 20% of the childcare workers should be men.

The activities of the Childcare Network were terminated in 1996, It is undoubtedly to the credit of the Network that it succeeded in putting the gender theme on the agenda of the EU Member States. Thanks to the work of this Network, European funding was made available to undertake actions to make provisions for young children in Europe more male-friendly. The European Social Fund, in particular, has financed numerous projects in various European countries in order to bring the gender balance in the facilities into equilibrium and in which the aim was to provide a gender-neutral structure of professionalism in the professions dealing with young children.

The influx of the necessary employees in the future can also be hypothecated by the extreme gender segregation in the sector. Women are becoming increasingly better educated and will, therefore, make other professional choices in the future. Various authors warn that it is less evident now that women will choose to go into the care professions. The safeguarding of a sufficient influx in childcare therefore demands – alongside of better training and status in the profession – that the gender segregation is breached, so that men will also start choosing jobs in the childcare sector (Cameron, Moss, 2007).

4.3. Origins of gender segregation in the provisions for young children

In 1995, and on commission from the Childcare Network of the European Commission, Fred Deven, a member of the Childcare Network, did a study of the number of men employed in childcare in Flanders. Of the 14,560 people who then worked in the Flemish childcare sector (0 to 3 years old), there were, all told, 81 men. This comes to 0.55% or one man to 200 women. He differentiated between childcare in facilities (day-care centres) where 1.5% of the staff were men, and the family day care sector that was apparently almost exclusively the terrain of women (0.1%). In Denmark, it was slightly better, with 5% employed for the 0 to 3 year-olds. The city of Barcelona was not doing a bad job, with 4%. Sweden had 3% for the 0 to 6-year old group and, in Finland, 4% worked with the age group 0 to 7. In the United Kingdom, ECEC was the most gender-segregated profession with only 2% for the 0 to 6-year olds. (Jensen, 1998: 126).

We can argue that childcare – and, also, kindergarten – is an explicitly female profession in all countries. Over the past few years, various authors have tried to find an answer to the question of why so few men work in the childcare professions. Below, we have listed the reasons.

4.3.1. Historic connection with the women's movement

We have determined that, in all the professions dealing with children, women are in the majority and the degree of gender segregation is in direct relation to the age of the children: the younger the children, the higher the percentage of women (Moss, 2003).

Moreover, childcare has always been an important item within the feminist movement (Desmet, et al., 1978; Pot, 1981; Farquhar, 2006:5). 'Early childhood services have always been promoted by women, used by women and worked in by women' (Farquhar, 2006:3). The women's emancipation movement has, in many industrialized countries, had an important impact on the increase of professionalism in childcare, as well as on the increase of the salaries. Up until the end of the 1980s, childcare was strongly linked with the women's movement which, on the one hand, aimed to give women the chance to work outside the home by providing more childcare but, on the other hand, also wanted to employ women in that sector (Farquhar, 2006). This solidarity with the feminist movement is given by Farquhar as one of the reasons why practically no men have followed the path into the childcare sector.

4.3.2. Women's professions are not attractive for men

Women are attracted to men's professions because they have a great deal to offer: more prestige, better salaries and more extensive career possibilities, but men who chose the traditional women's professions have less to gain and must generally make large sacrifices with respect to salary and status. 'Men in non-traditional occupations have less to gain and much to lose: sacrifice in terms of pay and status, as well as raising questions on masculinity and suitability for the job' (Simpson, 2005: 364). Farquhar phrased it even more sharply: 'Men who enter paid childcare work are often thought of as men who are not 'real' men or gay' (Farquhar, 2006: 6). The link between homosexuality and the choice for a profession in childcare has not yet been studied. Simpson has done this for other typically female professions. From Simpson's study, it appears that homosexual men have fewer problems holding their own in typically female professions and that they have fewer identity problems than heterosexual men when working in a primarily female environment (Simpson, 2005:377).

Salary and working conditions play an important role, but are still not the most important reasons. In countries with a high degree of professionalization, such as New Zealand, Sweden and also in the Flemish kindergarten – where salaries are equal to those in elementary and secondary education – we still see that the employment rate of men is low (Farquhar, 2006; Cameron, 2006).

4.3.3. Fear of being accused of being a paedophile

Fear of being accused of sexual abuse plays a role, in particular, in the Anglo-Saxon countries (Rolfe, 2005: 27). 'All women are perceived to be safe to work with young children whereas any man is considered suspect if he goes for this type of work' (Farquhar, 2006: 6). The fear of being accused of sexual abuse is, in a number of countries – including New

Zealand – the reason why men are discouraged from choosing a job that involves young children. Farquhar explained the connection between paedophile scandals and the absence of men. In New Zealand, in the 1990s, the percentage of men dropped from 2 to 1% after a case of sexual abuse that was extensively publicized in the gutter press (Farquhar, 2006). A study by the Day Care Trust in the UK brought to light that 57% of the group of adults questioned reported that the risk of paedophilia was a barrier to hiring more men for the childcare professions (Rolfe, 2005:14). In Denmark, and also in Flanders, the fear of being unjustly accused of abuse is much less alive (Jensen, 1998; Peeters, 2003).

4.3.4. Childcare is seen as woman's work

The primary reason for the great majority of women in the professions concerning young children can be found, according to various authors, in the fact that childcare is seen as 'women's work' (Cameron, Moss, Owen, 1999, Cameron, 2001: 449; Farquhar, 2006, 5). Childcare is seen as a replacement for the mother's role. Cameron, Moss and Owen use the concept of 'gender': the various characteristics and skills that are ascribed by a culture to men and women. Gender differentiates itself from sex which refers solely to the biological differences between men and women. According to Dejonckheere en Demuynck (2001: 7), 'gender and sex are strongly linked to each other by the fact that the biologically-determined sex will define which gender role (masculine or feminine) society expects a person to play. Because it is all about a social construction, gender is strongly susceptible to change: the differences between men and women will vary according to place, culture, ethnicity and class. 'Gender would, according to Cameron, Moss and Owen (1999) be unconsciously imbedded in the construction of professionalism for occupations dealing with young children. Caring for children – paid or unpaid – is experienced as women's work, something that women, by nature, do better. This gender mechanism operates on two levels. At the individual level, the childcare staff members bring, via their own gender identity, specific opinions as to how professionalism in the childcare sector must be interpreted: the role, tasks and behaviours of men and women in the specific context of the work in childcare. The gender component also plays a role in the institutional sphere: it has its impact on the historical origin of childcare and on the manner in which childcare is organised (the professionalism of the organisation). The gender aspect has, therefore, also been a determining factor in the policy of the government and the educational practices of the organised childcare facilities (professionalism of the activities). Childcare is, after all, inspired by a certain kind of care, namely maternal care. This is, according to various authors, the primary reason for the extremely limited number of men in the childcare sector (Cameron, Moss, Owen, 1999:8; Cameron, 2001: 449; Peeters, 2005a; Farquhar, 2006: 5).

4.3.5. Gender segregation reproduces itself

An additional reason why the childcare sector is so gender-segregated lies in the fact that a sector that is so strongly dominated by women reproduces the gender segregation via the policy, the image of the profession, the training courses, the selection and the type of professionalism developed (Rolfe, 2005). If we want to have a more gender-neutral form of professionalism, then action must be undertaken on all of these different levels. 'What needs to be more thoroughly examined is how curricula, organization and promotion of training for care work act as a gendered deterrent or stimulus, addressing the question of whether men are being implicitly kept out of care work' (Cameron, Moss, 2007: 119).

4.4. Working towards a gender-neutral concept of professionalism

If we want to achieve a gender-neutral concept of professionalism in working with young children, then we must rethink the structure of professionalism and it must be uncoupled from the mother-replacement concept (Cameron, Moss, Owen, 1999:25). A professionalism that originates from the replacement of the mother is based on a single stereotype classical gender identity. The classic gender identities are constructed on the basis of differences. They are based on the labelling of the other as different, and employ, therefore, the concept of exclusion: 'a man is different than a woman' (EC Network on Childcare, 1993). In order to avoid this exclusion, a model of professionalism must be constructed that is based on 'multiplicity of gendered identities' (Cameron, Moss and Owen, 1999: 20). Vandenbroeck (1999: 35) translates it as 'multiple identity': we must do away with a structure of professionalism that is based on one identity (be it gender, culture or ethnicity). There are various visions, various ways of working that are used by various people and that are all valuable and that can, therefore also be verified. Every interpretation of professionalism must be continually questioned and made transparent through dialogue and debate.

4.5. Conclusion: conditions for gender neutral professionalism

In order to be able to realize a gender neutral concept of professionalism, the climate in the training courses and the facilities must change. 'This revealing of the childcare workplace as a 'gendered' institution employing gendered discourses could envisage a different early childhood professional, one doing complex work in a modern and uncertain world where meanings are continually negotiated between children and adults and among adults' (Cameron, 2006: 77). The presence of male staff members and the active involvement of fathers in the facilities are essential conditions for achieving a gender neutral structure of professionalism. A gender neutral professionalism can, after all, only develop through critical reflection and discussion between the male and the female staff members and with the fathers and mothers.

Initiatives to attract more male staff members must, therefore, be encouraged but will, in the near future, not produce any spectacular results because qualified male childcare workers are simply not available on the labour market (Rolfe, 2005:3). It is, therefore, exceedingly important to develop the initial training courses based on a gender neutral professionalism and to focus actions on training courses that lead to professions in childcare.

An important role is reserved here for the centres that concentrate on choice of studies and vocational guidance. Men, in particular, who are dissatisfied with their current jobs (rethought career) and had been active in the past in child welfare work, should be alerted to opportunities offered by adult education.

Moreover, action must be taken to better counsel male adolescents in their study choices. In particular, those who are interested in working with children and young people should be brought into contact, via job fairs, with male childcare workers who can point out the creative opportunities of a job with children (Rolfe 2005). 'Men-only' orientation courses have proven to be extremely successful in bringing men to the initial training courses (Spence, 2007). The 'Men in Childcare' project in Scotland has, via this men-only orientation course, already brought in 900 men to an initial training course.

Networks of male students and childcare staff members, which already exist in Ireland, Norway, Scotland and New Zealand – among other places – are important in convincing young men to enter a training course or to prevent the men who have taken the step to train as childcare workers – or who already work in childcare – from dropping out. Via chat forums on the internet, these networks can reach isolated male students and childcare workers. Research has shown, moreover, that they are extremely popular among the users (Mannaert, 2006; Vandenheede, 2006).

The training courses for the childcare professions must be integrated in the training institutes where both 'typically male' – generally technical – and 'typically female' professions are taught. (Vandenheede, 2006). Schools must actively recruit male teachers and training supervisors. Male students should preferably be supervised by male supervisors or mentors.

A study by Vereecke (2006) demonstrated that, in the Childcare training course, there is – at least in Flanders – a hidden curriculum. The teaching materials reflect a 'feminine' professionalism. A screening for the gender neutrality of the course material that is used in the training courses appears to be essential in order to avoid this 'gender bias' as much as possible and to achieve a gender neutral interpretation of the courses.

Professionalism in the childcare professions should be given a broader interpretation. In countries such as Norway and Denmark, where a great deal of emphasis is placed on outdoor activities and sports, we find that a different type of professionalism is created that is gender neutral and, therefore, more attractive for male staff members and fathers (Wohlgemuth, 2003; Hauglund, 2005). Also, a structure of professionalism in which the social function of childcare has been strongly developed (Vandenbroeck, 2004) offers the opportunity to attract more men (Meleady, Broadhead, 2002).

The childcare facilities and schools must adapt the infrastructure and the working conditions to the male staff members and male students who are doing internships (no aprons, higher changing tables, toilet facilities) (Mannaert 2006; Vandenheede, 2006).

The offer of part-time jobs is a clear pull factor in the employment of men in jobs in childcare (Rolfe, 2005; Peeters, 2005). In the sectors such as out-of-school care, where there is a great deal of part-time work, one could look for a combination with other jobs so that full-time employment could be realized.

From the experiences in the Scandinavian countries, it is clear that actions to employ more men in the provisions for young children are only effective if they step in at all levels, and then over a long period of time. In order to bring more equilibrium into the gender balance, the political will is necessary to make this theme a policy priority for at least 10 years (Moss, 2003c). Governmental support of all kinds of actions and campaigns is, according to Moss, an important stipulation for success. In their policy documents, the government should continually mention the importance of the presence of men in the provisions for young children.

5

An international perspective on professionalism in Early Childhood Education and Care

5.1. Methodology

The co-constructing of knowledge by the mutual sharing of understandings is not simply a work method by which 'reflective practitioners' learn from each other. From a macro-perspective, countries can also – by 'listening' to each other's understandings – start to question the policy visions that they had assumed to be self-evident and start to accumulate new knowledge on the manner in which professionalism can be defined. 'It should enable us to understand better the social, cultural and political origins of our understandings, and to recognize that using evidence always means interpretation' (Moss, 2005: 3). This section of the study begins with the analysis of understandings that have been brought to the forefront in recent surveys on the interpretation of professionalism in the professions concerning young children in the industrialized countries. (Oberhuemer, Ullich, 1997; Oberhuemer, 2000, 2005; OECD, 2001, 2006; Bennett, 2003; Moss, 2003c; Cohen, Moss, Petrie, Wallace, 2004; Cameron, 2005; Cameron, Moss, 2007). In our analysis, we are going to examine how one deals with the policy paradox in the discourse on professionalism in the countries belonging to the Organization for Economic Cooperation and Development (OECD) and/or the European Union. This analysis also includes the results of the EQUAL project 'Improving Childcare,' financed by the European Social Fund, in which organizations belonging to the French-language Community – Belgium, Luxemburg, Italy, Germany, Lithuania and Flanders – took part. These countries, just as Flanders, are confronted with a policy paradox concerning the professionalism of professions dealing with young children. For three years, we worked together within this EQUAL project, in a workgroup on the theme of Professionalism in the professions for services for young children. The reports by the countries participating in this project

– the French-language Community of Belgium, Italy, Luxemburg and Flanders – can be found on www.vbjk.be/Improving Childcare. This group of countries is, at the moment, in the midst of a process of professionalization and various efforts are being made by actors in the field to find a solution for the policy paradox. The governments of these countries have, however, not yet outlined a coherent policy on the manner in which that professionalism is to be interpreted.

We will then do a more detailed study of Flanders, a EU Member State which is counter-acting this evolution: for the past 25 years, the Flemish childcare sector has been under-going a process of deprofessionalization.

Then we will study four countries which were selected because they, according to the international surveys, have developed an 'interesting practice and policy' with respect to professionalism. If our aim is to construct as much new knowledge as possible, it is important to focus our attention on those countries that have gone through develop-mental processes that have led to the most innovative understandings concerning profes-sionalism.

In this section, we use a literature study as well as interviews with 14 'key-persons' from the research and training world who are deeply involved in the debate on professionaliza-tion in their countries. These key-persons come from 9 different countries: New-Zealand, the French-language Community of Belgium, France, Denmark, England, Germany, Lux-emburg and Italy. We have selected academics and trainers who play important roles in their own countries or internationally in the debate on professionalization.

The following academics were interviewed: Dr. Florence Pirard, pedagogic advisor of ONE (governmental organisation of the French-language community in Belgium); Dr. Christa Preissing (Freie Universität Berlin Germany); Prof. Pat Broadhead (Leeds Metropolitan University, UK); Prof. Chris Pascal and Prof. Tony Bertram (Centre for Research in Early Childhood; University of Worcester, UK), Prof. Peter Moss (London University TCRC, UK); Tullia Musatti (University of Rome, Italy) and Prof. Carmen Dalli (Victoria University, Wellington, NZ).

The following training experts were selected: Sue Cherrington, Head of the School for Early Childhood Teacher Education (New Zealand); Myriam Mony, director of ESSSE, training institute for *éducateur jeunes enfants* (France); Anke van Keulen, director of a training organization (MUTANT) and former coordinator of the European Trainers Net-work DECET (The Netherlands); Jos Noessen, affiliated as pedagogue with the *Service de la Formation Professionelle* of the *Ministère de l' Education* (Luxemburg); Gill Haynes, representative of the National Childminding Organisation in the Children's Workforce Development Council (UK); Paul Ennals, Chief Executive of the National Children's Bureau and chairman of the Children's Workforce Network (UK); Dr. Richard Dorrance, director of Cache, the Council for Awards in Children's Care and Education and Sue Owen, Early Childhood Unit director of the National Children's Bureau (UK).

5.2. A tendency towards a broader interpretation of professionalism in the provisions for the youngest children

5.2.1. Opportunities for professionalization in integrated systems

Authors who have mapped out the Early Childhood systems in Europe and in the OECD countries differentiate between the so-called 'split systems' and 'integrated systems' (Oberhuemer, Ullich, 1997; Bennett, 2003; Moss, 2003; Oberhuemer, 2005; OECD, 2001, 2006). The split system model, in which childcare for the youngest children (under 3 or 4 years old) and the kindergarten are separate, is a common system in Europe: it exists in Belgium, France, Italy, Luxemburg, Portugal, Greece and Ireland. In Denmark, Finland, Sweden, New Zealand, Spain and, recently, also in England and Scotland, policy-makers have developed an integrated system by which the provisions for children between the ages of 0 and 4 are integrated into either the educational system – as in New Zealand, Spain, England, Scotland and Sweden – or a broader 'pedagogic' system such as in Finland and Denmark (Cohen, Moss, Petrie, Wallace, 2004; Moss, 2005). The integrating of childcare into a broader entity assumes an integrated structure and a common approach with respect to access, subsidies, curriculum and personnel. (Moss, 2005:4). Various authors have indicated that this differentiation between a 'split system' and an integrated system has important consequences for the professionalism of the staff members who work with the youngest children (0 to 3-4 years old) (Oberhuemer, 2000, 2005; Bennett, 2005; Moss, 2005; OECD, 2001, 2005). According to the OECD report, it is typical for the 'split regimes' that highly qualified and well-paid teachers work in the kindergartens, while the childcare for the 0 to 3-year old age group is done by low-schooled or non-qualified personnel who are, moreover, paid a great deal less. (OECD, 2006: 161). 'Early childhood educators working closest to the school gate are better trained and rewarded' (OECD, 2006: 158). The OECD has ascertained that there is a tendency to require a bachelor's diploma for those who work with children over the age of three. In some countries, such as France, The Netherlands and Ireland, this is the same training as for the elementary school teacher; in Belgium, Luxemburg and Greece, the training course for pre-school teacher is a specialized one for the 2.5 to 6-year olds.

'In services for the younger children, it is difficult to identify across the different countries (with a split system) a core professional who works directly with infants and toddlers. In many countries, childcare services tend to remain hierarchical with a few professionals (often trained nurses) managing the majority auxiliary staff who care for and interact with children' (OECD, 2006: 161). The explanation for these low qualifications in childcare is, according to the OECD, to be clarified by the vision that working with the youngest children is limited to physical care, a task that can be carried out by any woman without training. (OECD, 2006: 63). According to a recent OECD calculation, the salaries in the childcare sector (in a split system) are only 50 à 75 % of a teacher's salary. (OECD, 2006: 164).

The exception to the rule is France, a country with a distinct 'split system,' where, due to a specific history, a specialized training course was developed (*éducateur jeunes enfants*) for working with the youngest children based on a social pedagogy concept (Verba, 2006). This makes the French system extremely interesting for countries such as Belgium, with a 'split system'; for that reason, we will do an extensive study of the French system.

Cameron and Moss have determined that a growing number of countries are evolving in the direction of a more integrated approach in the provisions for children in the 0 to 6 age group. The care for the young child is being integrated into a broader entity of social welfare activities: 'pedagogy'. 'We see that there is an evolution that 'care' disappears as a distinctive policy and occupational field and becomes one part of another field: childcare being absorbed into 'education' in some cases, childcare and 'social care' into 'pedagogy' in others. Indeed, a continuing understanding of the field as 'care work' may be at odds with the objective of developing good quality employment, since work labelled 'care work' tends to be mired in poor conditions and low status' (Cameron, Moss, 2007:10). In these countries with an integrated model for services for children between 0 and 6 years old, a common professional profile originated: 'a single 'core' profession working in all early childhood centre-based services' (Moss, 2005: 4). These educators for young children – also called 'pedagogues' after the Danish '*pedagog*' – received training at the level of a professional bachelor's degree ('tertiary trained') (Oberhuemer, 2005: 9). In these integrated models, these bachelors work together with trained 'child assistants' (generally at the level of secondary technical or professional education) who primarily take on the care tasks. (OECD, 2006: 161).

Within the integrated system, there are, however, also large differences. In Denmark and Finland, the provisions for young children and the after-school care are integrated into the Social Welfare sector, and the *pedagog* is the primary professional in these facilities (Moss, 2005: 3). Because the Danish *pedagog* professional has been able to develop a singular and fascinating interpretation of professionalism, we will study the Danish model in great detail in a separate chapter.

The 'early childhood teacher/pedagogue' is, in the countries with an integrated system, the most common professional. There are, however, differences with respect to the ages of the children for whom they are responsible. In New Zealand, it is the intention of the 'Ten Years Strategic Plan for ECE' that, by 2012, all staff members who work with children between the ages of 0 to 5, will have a teaching qualification at the bachelor level. In Spain, the *'Maestro de EGB especialista en educacion infantil'* care for children up to the age of 6 (Balaguer, 2003:22), and, in Sweden, the teacher works with children up to the age of 12 (Johansson, 2003:24). England is a separate case within this category with its 'Early Years Professional Role,' a title which one can earn via various paths within the National Qualifications Framework and that does not refer to obtaining a diploma. For the Belgian context, the models of New Zealand and England are particularly interesting; we will, therefore, discuss these systems extensively. The New Zealand model is, namely, based on an expansion of the kindergarten to the 0 to 3-year old group and, since the kindergarten in Belgium has been vigorously expanded (OECD, 2006), this 'Kiwi' model offers a number of inspiring perspectives. The English system of National Vocational Qualifications Framework allows access via various paths of study and via the recognition of earlier acquired competencies that allow non-qualified or low-schooled candidates to go onto the teacher qualification programme (Early Years Professional Role). The system of recognition of earlier acquired competencies is, at the moment, on the rise (Peeters, 2005). We will, therefore, investigate the English system in a separate chapter.

5.2.2. Push and pull factors for professionalism within a 'split system'

The split model has a number of disadvantages: parents must pay a contribution for the care of their youngest children, which limits the accessibility to certain social groups; the salary and education are lower, and there is less attention to pedagogy and more to para-medical traditions (Oberhuemer, Ulich, 1997: 8). According to Oberhuemer, the disadvantages of a 'split system' are magnified even more in the private commercial sector. 'The market model of childcare, in particular, generates highly differentiated systems of training, payment and employment conditions' (Oberhuemer, 2005: 8). Commercial childcare businesses are driven by market forces and they will attempt to bring down labour costs at the expense of quality. In doing this, they only take into account the minimum quality requirements and, moreover, only pay minimum wages (OECD, 2006: 168).

Linda Mitchell did a meta-analysis of studies in various industrialized countries in which 'private and community-based childcare' systems were compared to each other. She concluded that the commercial sector scored lower with respect to the training level and salaries of the staff members (Mitchell, 2002:2). Mitchell argued, therefore, that it is essential that the government take measures to upgrade the qualifications of the staff members in the private commercial sector (Mitchell, 2002:13).

A number of countries, including the French-language Community of Belgium and The Netherlands, have already taken measures in that sense. In The Netherlands, where the entire childcare sector has been 'market-driven' since 2005, diploma requirements have been set that are comparable to those in the official day-care centres in Flanders.

The French-language Community also sets the same qualification requirements for the commercial child-care centres as for the official, subsidized day-care centres (Pirard, 2007:09:00). It is, however, striking that the Flemish government does not set any qualification requirements for the independent day-care centres in Flanders and Brussels and, in the mini-crèches, only those in positions of authority are required to have a secondary diploma that is equivalent to 'Childcare' if the organisation wants to apply for an annual subsidy of 500 euros per child per year.

In countries where no qualification requirements have been set for the independent sector, the salaries are low, as well. In the United States, where market-driven childcare is the rule, the childcare worker earns less than a garbage man or an assistant undertaker. (OECD, 2006: 169). In Flanders, there is no information available concerning the salaries of the childcare workers in the private sector.

Cameron and Moss point out the negative effects that a 'market approach' can have on the professional satisfaction of the childcare staff members. In a commercial, market-driven approach, the care of children is divided into fragmented tasks that can be bought by the consumers as separate services (for example, evening/night care via service vouchers). Because of this, a 'taylorisation of services' is created, such that the commercial provider feels necessitated to apply methods of control and supervision to the care-givers that, in turn, undermine the motivation of the care-givers. 'Many care workers today have poor employment conditions, yet they report considerable satisfaction with their work because of the autonomy they enjoy and their sense that the work is meaningful and socially important. But can either autonomy or meaning be sustained if the work is increasingly commodified and controlled through managerial technologies and market disciplines? Does this lead to a potentially damaging conflict of values and rationalities?' (Cameron, Moss, 2007: 152).

In a 'split system', the professionalization process has the greatest chance in a sector steered and subsi*dized by* the government (Oberhuemer, 2005). France, Belgium and Luxembourg are examples of countries with a 'split system' in which a portion of the sector is controlled by the government.
Of these countries, France has achieved the most progress in the area of professionalism. French childcare, just as Belgian childcare, has evolved from a paramedical tradition with paediatric nurses running the facilities (*puéricultrices*) and childcare workers (*auxiliaires de puériculture*) at the level of secondary professional education. Starting in 1993, there has been a clearly noticeable evolution with respect to attracting specialized educators with a social pedagogic background. The training course *éducateur jeunes enfants* has been a professional bachelor's course since 2005 .
Luxemburg offers an interesting model, because the *éducateur gradué* – who has a bachelor's diploma as a carer of children, handicapped persons and the elderly – can also be employed for the 5 and 6-year olds in the schools (Noesen, 2007). One strength for Belgium is that both the French-speaking and the Dutch-speaking Communities have at their disposal what the OECD calls 'the governance structures necessary for system accountability and quality assurance' (OECD, 2006: 208). L'Office de la Naissance et de l'Enfance and Kind en Gezin [Child and Family] are powerful government organizations that are also able to actually implement the qualification requirements that have been set by the government.

5.2.3. A generic or a specialistic type of professionalism

In its conclusions, the European 'Care Work in Europe' project states that important choices will have to be made in the future in many countries with a low level of professionalism. Thus, these countries will have to choose between 'a generalist and a specialist professional' (Cameron, Moss, 2007: 144).

In the 'specialist professional' model, specialized professionals work together with various types of assistants. This model is characterized by a more differentiated and hierarchical labour structure. In some sectors, we only find those with a bachelor's degree in management or training functions and they generally do not work with the children. These tasks are reserved for the assistants with a secondary education.

The professionalism in this model is linked to a specific age group or to specific services or policy domains and there is less of a holistic and domain-exceeding approach than in the following model. When the untrained also work there, their tasks are described in terms of concrete professional skills and competencies. The French system is an example of this model with a 'specialist professional': the *éducateur jeunes enfants*.

The second model is based on a communal holistic approach ('pedagogy' or social welfare approach) that places the accent on the interactional aspect of the work and not on the performance of concrete tasks. Generic professionalism encompasses an initial training course at the level of a professional bachelor's degree. This professional is trained to take on all aspects of the work, from the day-to-day care and education of children to management functions. He/she is aided in this by a generic professional who has been educated at the level of higher secondary education. Both types of generic professionals are prepared to work with various age groups and in various institutional contexts (young children, after-school care, residential care and youth welfare). The most explicit example of a generic professional is the Danish *pedagog*.

5.2.4. The necessity for a bachelor's training course

In Chapter 3, it was established that many authors agree that 'work in the care work domain is becoming more complex and demanding and getting more so; being a woman or having been a housewife is not a sufficient basis for undertaking such work today, if it ever was' (Cameron, Moss, 2007: 154). In order to be able to handle these complex tasks, Early Childhood Education needs a professional who is a co-constructor of knowledge, a critical thinker and a reflective and democratically focused practitioner. For that reason, we need a generically trained 'pedagogue', teacher or educator at the bachelor's level, who works together with assistants who have, at the very least, a diploma at the level of higher secondary education (Cameron, Moss, 2007: 12).

In Flanders, the research world has been advocating a bachelor's level training course for childcare for 30 years (Van Kordelaar, 1976; De Backer, 1973; Stellemans, 1976; WOVO, 1979; Baekelmans, 1993), but the political world did not comply with this request. In February 2007, a 'Taskforce Integrated Competency Policy for Childcare' was set up by the Minister of Welfare in collaboration with the Minister of Employment and Social Economics. In this Taskforce, it was determined that the tasks of the childcare worker would be expanded by the innovations that had recently been implemented in the childcare sector (Centra voor Kinderopvang [Centres for Childcare]). Therefore, the taskforce, in its meeting of June 2007, studied the necessity for having a number of childcare workers with a bachelor's degree (Taskforce, 2007).

According to Pirard, in the French-language Community nearly everyone in the sector agrees that the level of the *puéricultrice* (seventh-year level professional education, just as in Flanders) must be upgraded. Due to economic reasons, that has thus far not happened (Pirard, 2007). The OECD also blames economic motives for the reason why the educational level has not yet been upgraded in a small number of countries (OECD, 2007: 168).

In this, Belgium is not following the tendency that can be observed in most of the countries to create, alongside of the secondary professional education, a bachelor's training course. In Italy, alongside of the training course *educatrice asilo nido* at the level of secondary education, they have also recently instigated a bachelor's training course (Musatti, 2007: 10:00).

In Germany, the training for *Erzieherin* is, just as in Flanders, a course at the technical level. Three years ago, the discussion concerning the necessity for a bachelor's training course was started and, at the time of the interview with Christa Preissing (August 2007), 25 schools of higher professional education were already offering a bachelor's degree course. According to Preissing, it is not certain what the effect will be of the influx of these bachelor graduates into the workforce. She suspects that many of these graduates will continue their education and go on to achieve a Master's degree and that, especially during the first few years, they will take on management and counseling functions. Whether or not, in the future, the *Erzieherinnen* with a bachelor's diploma will also be employed to work with children, will depend upon whether or not higher salaries will also be paid for these functions (Preissing, 2007:04:23). Mathias Urban also has questions concerning the lack of a common curriculum for the course and questions whether or not the course dovetails sufficiently well with the innovations that have been instigated in the sector over the past few years (Urban, 2007). One of the examples of such an innovation is the curriculum for the province of Berlin that is based on the concept of *Bildung*. *Bildung* is the activity of the child by which he/she develops a vision of the world in his own tempo. This Berlin 'Bridging Diversity an Early Childhood Curriculum' is also innovative because of the importance that is attached to respect for diversity (Prott, Preissing, 2007).

Luxemburg has had a bachelor's training course for some time now: '*éducateur gradué*', '*Erzieher*'. This professional can be – like the Danish *pedagogue* – employed in a wide variety of functions: for the youngest children, both in the crèches and in the *maisons relais* (integrated centres), in the schools (5 to 6-year olds), but also for children and adults with special needs and the elderly. The *éducateur gradué* stands for a social-educational interpretation of professionalism (Noesen, 2007).

In the following chapters, we will see that France (*éducateur jeunes enfants*) and England (*Early Years Professional Role*) also have training courses at the bachelor level.

The Netherlands, a country with a 'split system' in which the childcare workers are trained at the secondary level (SPW 3), does not have a training course at the bachelor's level. A new training course, SPW 4, was started. It consists of one year after secondary school. A new bachelor course, 'Pedagogical management', will be set up in autumn 2008. Belgium (both Communities) and The Netherlands appear to be the only countries in this group of Western European countries (France, England, Germany, Italy, Luxemburg) that have not yet taken the initiative to create a training course for childcare at the bachelor's level.

In a number of countries, the training course is organized at the university level: the Förskollärare/Fritidspedagog in Sweden, the 'qualified teacher' in the United Kingdom, 'social pedagogues' in Finland and the *Educatore de Infancia* in Portugal. The authors of the OECD report Starting Strong, have found that the introduction of university diplomas for working with children has been met with a great deal of resistance from the national governments. The fear exists that childcare will, because of this, become too expensive and that this will hinder the necessary increase of places in the near future. But also, many experienced trainers in the countries that were studied fear that a university training course would be too theoretical: 'It may not practice an experiential and co-constructive model of education, suitable for work with young children' (OECD,

2006, 168). Tullia Musatti also has her doubts about possibly making a university diploma compulsory in Italy. The Italian university pedagogical training would not be sufficiently connected to the specific culture of Early Childhood Education (Musatti, 2007, 10:00; Improving Childcare, 2007).

Preissing regrets that, in Germany, the link between research and practice is extremely weak. *Erzieherinnen* should, she feels, be given the opportunity to become involved in action research projects in order to help bridge the gap between research and practice. (Preissing, 2007: 07:06).

Alongside of this, there is, in many countries, the necessity for a training course for the leaders or directors/managers. This necessity is present in the French-language Community where there is no specialized training course for those in positions of authority. Flanders has a post-bachelor course '*Verantwoordelijke Kinderopvang*' [Leadership of Childcare provisions] that is being instigated in Gent and Antwerp, but there is, as yet, no initial training course for managers.

We can conclude that there is a broad consensus that – also within the facilities for the youngest children – some of the staff members who work with the children should have a bachelor's degree. The question, however, remains unanswered concerning which type of training course is appropriate. On the basis of a cross-national study of training courses in Early Childhood Education in various countries, Oberhuemer has made a differentiation among four types of professional roles at the bachelor level (Ullich, Oberhuemer, 1997; Oberhuemer: 2000; 2005). We used this classification and added a number of new professional roles from countries that were not included in the Oberhuemer study (Oberhuemer, 2000: 2).

The early years childhood pedagogue/ teacher	Children from birth to compulsory school age	New Zealand (Early childhood education teacher) Spain (*maestro de EGB especialista en educacion infantil*) UK (early years professional role)
Preschool specialist/ teacher	The two or three years preceding primary school entry	Belgium (*institutrice/instituteur de maternelle/kleuterleid(st)er*) Luxembourg (*instituteur/institutrice de l'éducation préscolaire*) Greece (*nipiagogos*)

Teacher	Nursery and primary education (age range 2-12)	France (*professeur des écoles*) 2-12 Ireland (national teacher) The Netherlands (*leraar basisonder-wijs*) 4-8 Sweden (0-12)
Social pedagogue	Various fields including early childhood education	Denmark (*pedagog*) (age range 0-99) Germany (*Erzieher/Erzieherin*) (age range 0-14) Luxemburg (*educateur /éducatrice*) (for work with all ages outside the education system) France (*éducateur jeunes enfants*) (specialised in all social work (also childcare) with young children and their parents - childcare centres (0-3)

Even in this classification, we acknowledge that, within one specific professional role, there are great differences with respect to the interpretation of professionalism. Thus, the professionalism of the Swedish teacher is based on a holistic approach to the child, which is a far cry from the French *instituteur*, who is a proponent of a formal learning-based interpretation of professionalism (Bachelet, Mozère, 2004: 213).

5.2.5. The case of Flanders: a process of deprofessionalization

The professionalism of childcare in Flanders is characterized by a policy paradox by which the demands that are set for the profession have increased sharply while the access to the profession is, to an increasing degree, less guided by diplomas or certificates. A recent study showed that this policy paradox on professionalism in childcare professions in Flanders originated in the 1980s (Peeters, 2008). The cool, distant, technical professionalism that was based on a medical-hygienic 'meta-narrative', was criticized from within the academic world and, from research and the analysis of narratives (Peeters, 2008), it appeared that the parents were bothered by the chilly approach taken with their young children. Stimulated by, among other things, the Bernard van Leer Project 'Preschool Childcare in Gent' ['*Voorschoolse Opvang Gent*'] at the University of Gent, a counter-movement was instigated in 1979 that constructed a new interpretation of professionalism. This project influenced new regulations in 1983, which included an increase in the quality requirements with respect to parent participation. The pedagogic aspect gained importance in the quality requirements set by the government, but the training course 'Childcare' organized by the Department of Education was not fundamentally adapted, and the medical-hygienic aspect continued to dominate the training course and the sector. A study among parents (Baeyens, 1984) confirmed this dissatisfaction that the parents had with the detached care in the childcare facilities and concluded that parents would rather have their children cared for by family day carers than at childcare centres. The government used this study to allow the use of cheap care by family day carers – that thus far was viewed with suspicion because of the lack of training requirements – to grow exponentially. The sector of the 'non-qualified' family day carers expanded increasingly. By the late 1980s, the sector was dominated by a 'refresher course' optimism: there was a dominating conviction by the government, the researchers and the managing powers in the facilities that the professionalization problems could be eradicated through short refresher courses. The government promoted refresher courses, on the one hand for the childcare workers in order to adjust their initial medical-hygienic training and, on the other hand, for the family day carers in order to provide them with a certain degree of professionalism.

In the early 1990s, the government introduced the Scales for the Pedagogic Functioning of the Childcare Centres [*Schalen voor het Pedagogisch Functioneren van de Kinderdagverblijven*], based on the ITERS scale of Harms and Clifford (1980) by which the quality requirements were sharply upgraded. It was not until 1997 that the training course 'Childcare' – focusing on the hygienic aspects of care – was reformed and was extended by one year. This was, however, not sufficient to satisfy the demands that were set by the parents and by the governmental organisation Child and Family [*Kind en Gezin*]. The reform was not successful in forming 'reflective professionals' who would fulfil the new construction of professionalism as described in the literature. 'Childcare' remained a technical training course that was far removed from the reflective and action-based professionalism that was constructed by 'actors of change' within projects that were based at the University of Gent. Through the technical, static interpretation of professionalism, the 'Childcare' training course was not sufficiently successful in proving its added value with respect to the unschooled co-workers (family day carers and small commercial day care centres, called mini-crèches). This has contributed to the fact that, thus far, the paradox is continuing to grow.

Within the framework of the European projects in which the VBJK [Research and Resource Centre for Early Childhood Care and Education] and the Flemish governmental organisation Child and Family have assumed the role of promoter, didactical material was produced and initial training courses were developed for family day carers and staff members in out-of-school care programs. Moreover, a training course was also organized for managers of private childcare facilities and experiments were done with a qualifying training course within the framework of adult education.

The professionalization of the family day carers is a complex theme, as the family day carers themselves are divided on this question. One group of family day carers came into contact with the professionalization movement of family day carers in Scandinavia and the United Kingdom, and is working for an employees' statute. Another group, however, does not see this as a job, but as a temporary activity in which the motivation can be sought more in the opportunity to be able to care for one's own children than in an intrinsic interest in the job, itself. The family day carer statute was sensitively improved in 2003 but, from an inquiry in 2005 (Bettens, Buysse, Schroeikens, 2005), it became clear how divided the family day carers were about this new statute. Supported by the labor unions, one active group of family day carers continues to work for an employees' statute. They won the case in the Belgian Court of Cassation so that there is a realistic chance that the government, in time, will have to grant an employees' statute to the family day carers who are affiliated with a service. The creation of an employees' statute will probably scare off the group who sees the family day carer as a temporary activity and not as a profession. Moreover, this will have a negative effect on the costs of Flemish daycare, as an employees' statute would make childcare with family day carers expensive: they can, after all, care for fewer children at one time than a daycare centre. The withdrawal of one group of family day carers and the costs involved would have a negative effect on the entire amount of daycare in Flanders, since childcare by family day carers accounts for 54% of the childcare places.

The beginning of the new millennium is characterized by the growth of the private commercial day care centres. In 2001, the Minister of Welfare promotes, via a media campaign, the instigation of private mini-crèches, with the argument that they do not require any training. This campaign from the Welfare Ministry reinforced, in the public opinion, the image that only 'maternal' skills and competencies are important for a job in childcare.

5.2.5.1. A new dominant discourse

The Labor Department understands this signal from Welfare to be that the childcare sector would be the ideal way to help short-schooled, unemployed women find work.

Childcare professions are categorized with the technical working professions and, within the Labor Department and other organizations of employers and employees, a new dominant discourse arises, that is based on a static technical vision of professionalism.

The childcare worker would, in keeping with this dominant discourse, only have to possess simple working skills. In the meantime, Child and Family is taking the necessary measures to adapt childcare to the new demands from the society in general and the parents in particular.

The necessity for an initial training course at a higher level, because of the requirements that ensue from new quality regulations, such as the Quality Decree, and the setting up of pilot projects for multi-functional Integrated Centres for Childcare [*Centra voor Kinderopvang*], is becoming increasingly greater. The professionalism within the fastest growing segment of the sector, however, is cause for concern. The new childcare places are, to an increasing degree, being taken up by staff members who must work under extremely poor conditions: they work for a pittance and/or do not even have elementary rights as employees. Within the scientific world and within international organizations, there is a consensus that quality care cannot be realized under such miserable working conditions (OECD, 2006). Because of the acute shortage of childcare, the organizing powers, to an increasing degree, are outsourcing their childcare to private facilities, such that the professionalism of the childcare sector is declining and, in terms of percentages, an increasing number of unschooled workers are being employed. This makes the job less and less attractive and will, in time, according to labor sociologists, cause a scarcity in the labor market (Coomans, 2002). There is a real risk that there will be a shortage of childcare which, in times of an aging population when women are essential for the labor market, can have serious consequences for the economy (Cameron, Moss, 2007).

5.2.5.2. Professionalism as 'quality of action', or the search for action-oriented competencies

In the various types of care in Flanders (subsidized childcare centres, family day carers and private facilities), important work has been done by childcare workers on the construction of an evolutionary, democratic professionalism, based on a 'quality of action' (Oberhuemer, 2000). A recent study about those little narratives documents a pedagogical practice that is capable of coping with complex situations (Peeters, 2008). These 'actors of change' gained – within the action-research projects – action-oriented competencies that made it possible to change the existing practices (Cameron, Moss, 2007: 142; Rinaldi, 2006: 133). These action-oriented competencies are in sharp contrast with the technical-working competencies that were required from within the projects of the Labor Department and which are based on previously determined 'outcomes', the effect of which is that change and innovation are curbed and a mediocre quality is maintained.

As far as the professionalism of the directors or leaders of the childcare provisions is concerned, we see positive developments: in 2003, a new post-bachelor training course 'Leader of childcare provision' was started within the Associations University Gent and University Antwerp. The Schools for Higher Professional Education of Gent, are developing a modular system for the training course in Gent and in the training course in Antwerp, e-learning is of major importance. The University of Gent started an academic master's course 'Social Work' in which, for the first time in Flanders, the subject 'Childcare' is being taught at an academic level.

5.2.5.3. Conclusion: Flanders:
the only country in a spiral of deprofessionalization

In all of the countries that were studied, there was a process of professionalization, or such a process was being set up such that an investment was being made in the upgrading of qualifications and in better working conditions. Our study has shown that Flanders is counteracting this evolution: for the past 25 years, the Flemish childcare sector has been undergoing a process of deprofessionalization. Diploma requirements are being abandoned and an increasing number of short-schooled workers are finding employment in the sector. During the 1980s, this evolution was started by the spectacular increase of the services for family day carers. We have seen that, during the past few years, the process of deprofessionalization has again gained momentum, on the one hand because of the exponential growth of the mini-crèches – which have no diploma requirements – and, on the other hand, by the employment projects for short-schooled workers instigated by the Department of Employment and Social Economy.

The technical interpretation of professionalism within the secondary training course 'Childcare' is one of the causes of this process of deprofessionalization. The training course 'Childcare' has not been successful in convincing the parents and the policy-makers of the added value of this course and, based on this assessment, the importance of an initial training course for a profession with young children has been called into question.

Moreover, in the professions working with young children in Flanders, it is also not going well with another aspect of professionalism, namely the working conditions of the employees. The two sectors that are hardly growing at all, namely the childcare centres and the sector of the family day care services, have managed to improve the working conditions: a salary raise for the teachers and a better statute for the family day carers have been realized. The fastest-growing sector – that of the mini-crèches – on the other hand, is cause for great concern, since they are not financially viable (Misplon, et al., 2004). In this sector, fragmented, low-quality, poorly paid jobs are being created at a high tempo in which the statute of the employees – 'illegal-independent workers and personnel without an employee's contract' – (Misplon, et al., 2004: 103) – does not comply with the basic social rights of the employees. On top of that, there are no training or qualification requirements for this sector and there is little willingness seen for lifelong learning. Moreover, the HIVA-study has ascertained that there is an extremely large turnover of personnel (Misplon, et al., 2004: 54). In our study, we have extensively documented an extremely broad consensus, both in international organizations and in the scientific literature (OECD, 2006; Sylva, et al., 2004; Cameron, Moss, 2007), that this combination of low salaries, high work pressure, the lack of basic rights of the employee, the turnover of personnel, the lack of training requirements and a low willingness for lifelong learning are strong indicators for low pedagogic quality. An international comparative study (van Ijzendoorn, Tavecchio, Riksen-Walraeve, 2004) on the quality of care in the independent sector is, therefore, essential.

By this creating of low-quality jobs, Flanders is opposing the guidelines of the European Commission which, within the framework of its pursuit of a 'knowledge-based society' advocates 'Quality of Employment' (European Commission, 2005b: 2). The Organization for Economic Cooperation and Development (OECD, 2006) and labor sociologists (Coomans, 2002) warn against the creation of such low-quality jobs: such jobs give the sector a bad image and hypothecate the influx of workers in the sector for the future. Young women who enter the labor market are, after all, much more highly educated than the group of women leaving the labor market. It is, therefore, by no means certain that, in the future, this growing sector in childcare will be able to find sufficient employees for these low-quality jobs. A labor market shortage will slow down the necessary growth of childcare, which can have serious consequences for the employment of women, who are essential in the labor market in order to absorb the consequences of the aging population.

5.3. Recently developed coherent models of professionalism in the United Kingdom, France, New Zealand and Denmark

On the basis of the analysis of a number of important overview studies, a group of countries were chosen for which the government has instigated a coherent policy to upgrade the qualifications: England, France, New Zealand and Denmark. In these four countries, the government invested in increased professionalism, while the concrete interpretation of the type of professionalism differs for each of the four countries. The four different interpretations of professionalism are especially inspiring for other countries which are in the process of professionalization. As with the previous section of our study, we chose an approach for this section based on involvement with respect to the object of the research: 'Situatedness in a concrete social practice is not seen as a threat to independent judgement. On the contrary it is assumed that this is exactly what will raise the quality of judgement' (Dahlberg, Moss, 2005:75). One of the determining factors in our choice was whether or not we were sufficiently familiar with the practices in the chosen country; we determined this on the basis of structured cooperation with training and professional organisations in the chosen countries or regions that had been going on for at least three years. We studied three EU countries (Denmark, France and England) and New Zealand based on a vision of professionalism that we developed in Chapter 3, and that is based on a normative, evolutionary and participatory concept.

This section on the international perspective of professionalism was submitted to a 'key-person' from each country in question. This person checked the text for mistakes and faulty interpretations and, subsequently, the commentary of this 'key-person' was incorporated into the text.

5.4. England: working towards an integrated qualification framework

5.4.1. Methods followed

For the research of this section on the recent evolutions concerning professionalism in England, we set to work as follows. First of all, we did an extensive literature study of the recent evolution in the United Kingdom (Griffin, 1991; Moss, 1991; Oberhuemer, Ullich, 1997; Sylva, et al., 2004; Cameron, 2004; 2007; Moss, Petrie, 2002; Cohen, Moss, Petrie, Wallace, 2004; Pascal, Bertram, 2005, Moss, 2006; Osgood, 2006a; Miller, 2006). After consulting Linda Miller of the Open University and member of the Special Interest Group Professionalism of the European Early Childhood Education Research Association, we decided to make an exploratory visit to the London department of the Children's Workforce Development Council, together with a colleague, Geert Keersmaekers. The CWDC is the official organ that was commissioned by the government to implement the changes in the 'Children's Workforce'. The CWDC is a division of the Sector Skills Council, Skills for Care and Development. Then, Linda Miller was contacted once again with the request to select people who play a key role in the 'Children's Workforce' professionalization process for an interview.

The choice fell on Gill Haynes, representative of the National Child-minding Organisation in the 'Children's Workforce Development Council' (CWDC); Paul Ennals, Chief Executive of the National Children's Bureau and chairman of the Children's Workforce Network; Dr. Richard Dorrance, director of CACHE, the Council for Awards in Children's Care and Education and, finally, Sue Owen, Early Childhood Unit director of the National Children's Bureau, who has been following the evolution of the National Vocational Qualifications for years. On January 10 2007, these four individuals were interviewed in London. On February 3 2007, in-depth interviews were done in Birmingham with three scientists who had been keeping a close eye on the evolutionary changes: Prof. Tony Bertram, Prof. Chris Pascal and Prof. Pat Broadhead.

The choice was made in favour of Prof. Pat Broadhead (Leeds Metropolitan University) in her function as chairman of TACTYC, an early years national and international organisation supporting those who train early years educators in any capacity. She was, among other things, involved as a researcher in the evaluation of numerous programmes in Children's Centres and Sure Start programmes (Broadhead, Armistead, 2007). Prof. Chris Pascal and Prof. Tony Bertram were chosen as directors of CREC (Centre for Research in Early Childhood, University of Worcester). They received the research commission to evaluate the Early Excellence Centres. This study proved how important a qualified staff is (Pascal, Bertram, 2005).

5.4.2. Early Childhood Education is becoming a policy priority in England

5.4.2.1. Before 1997: the UK, Europe's weakling younger brother

When the Labour Party came to power in 1997, after years of a Conservative government, the United Kingdom was lagging way behind with respect to childcare provisions (childcare and kindergarten) in comparison with other European countries. In 1996, the United Kingdom had, for example, only 2% subsidized places (0 to three years old) at a time when Belgium had 30%.(European Commission Network on Childcare, 1996). Only 10% of the staff members in the provisions for young children (childcare and kindergarten) had a diploma (Owen en Haynes, 2007). Since 1997, they have, however, been making up for lost time. The British government is making important investments in the sector of provisions for young children while, at the same time, an innovative policy with respect to content is being initiated. The government has taken important initiatives to enable the integration of provisions for children and parents (the Children's Centres) and efforts are being made to achieve an Integrated Qualification Framework.

In the recent history of the provisions for young children in the United Kingdom, 1997 is a pivotal moment (Cohen, Moss, Petrie, Wallace, 2004: 51). Before New Labour came to power, childcare was seen as the responsibility of the parents. Cohen illustrates this with a quote from a British minister of the Conservative government: 'Our view is that it is for the parents who go out to work to decide how best to care for their children. If they want or need help in this task they should make the necessary arrangements and meet the costs' (Cohen, Moss, Petrie, Wallace, 2004: 53). The consequence of this neoliberal policy was that childcare, until 1997, mostly consisted of independent family day carers and a growing number of private, commercial day-care centres. These expensive commercial provisions were chiefly populated by children from dual-income families.

However, the Conservative government did vote for the Children's Act in 1989. This Children's Act stated that a small number of subsidized facilities (only 2% of the total number of children, the lowest number within the EU-12 in 1988) (Moss, 1991a) was to be reserved for 'children in need and their families'. Furthermore, the Children's Act was also to regulate the private commercial facilities (Cohen, Moss, Petrie, Wallace, 2004: 52). Oberhuemer en Ullich (1997:203) talk about a 'diverse and fragmented system of childcare and education services'. Others also emphasized the fragmentation and the lack of a coherent policy in the British system before 1997 (Moss, 1991b: 139; Cohen, Moss, Petrie, Wallace, 2004: 55). The authors describe the situation in 1997, at the beginning of the New Labour government, as follows:

'A split departmental responsibility between welfare, responsible for day care and child-care services and education (nursery and compulsory schooling); a fragmented body of services not only divided between the welfare and the education system, but with differ-ent types of services for different purposes and families; low levels of publicly funded childcare and early education and a growing marketisation of all services' (Cohen, Moss, Petrie, Wallace, 2004: 55-56).

5.4.2.2. After 1997: Early Childhood Education as the means for solving major social problems

The Labour government of Prime Minister Tony Blair, who came to power after the elec-tions of 1997, made childcare a political priority for the first time in post-war history (Cohen, Moss, Petrie, Wallace, 2004: 56). Early Childhood Education was seen as a provi-sion that could contribute to the realisation of a number of the government's important political targets: the reduction of poverty through the participation of single mothers in the labor market; the promotion of equality between men and women; a competitive labor market and an increased productivity (HM Treasury, 2000). Childcare and pre-school education are, in the vision of the British government, an important means of tackling the major social problems. Margareth Hodge[3], the later 'first ever Minister for Children, Young People & Families' (ePolitix.com, 2007), will have played an important role in putting ECE on the political agenda. She was able to convince HM Treasury's Vice-premier Gordon Brown that ECE was an important means of achieving objectives in the areas of poverty reduction and general employment (Cohen, Moss, Petrie, Wallace, 2004: 64). These political objectives were submitted to the National Childcare Strategy

---

3   Margareth Hodge concentrated, in her political career, on the emancipation of women. She became a Member of Parliament in 1994 and was, as a member of the Labour Shadow Cabinet, responsible for the writing of the Early Years Policy of the Labour Party (Under-5s policy). She did not immediately become a member of the government after the Labour take-over but continued, as an MP, to apply pressure to bring childcare under the Education umbrella. In 2003, she became the 'first ever Minister for Children, Young People and Families.'

in 1998: 'to ensure quality, affordable childcare for children aged 0 to 14 years in every neighbourhood' (DfEE, 1998, para 1.26). This Childcare Strategy endeavored to improve the quality of the provisions by also creating a new training and qualification framework and offering more opportunities for refresher and training courses for the staff members. Alongside of that, the 'National Childcare Strategy' wanted to make childcare more accessible and affordable, and to drastically increase the number of available places.

The United Kingdom had, just as in Belgium and France, a so-called 'split system' (OECD, 2001) for provisions for young children, by which childcare was placed under the authority of 'Welfare' and kindergarten was under the Ministry of Education. In early 1998, the new British government made the important decision to reform this 'split system' and to transfer the responsibility for childcare from Welfare to Education. This reform was inspired by the policy document that was written by Margareth Hodge in 1997 and on the many studies that were set up on this subject in the 1990s (Cohen, Moss, Petrie, Wallace, 2004: 64-65).

5.4.2.3. From 'Early Excellence Centres' to 'Children's centres': a new type of professionalism is formed

From 1997 to 1999, pilot projects were started for Early Excellence Centres (Pascal, Bertram, 2005: 174). The merging of the fragmented services was central to this innovation, with the intention to create a new dynamic in the sector. Services for childcare, pre-school educational facilities, centres for parenting support, centres for the training of long-term unemployed, health services and retraining centres for tutors all started to work together in these Early Excellence Centres (EEC).

From the evaluation, it became apparent that the EEC's had developed a new type of professionalism (of the activities) that were passed on as 'examples of good practice' via training courses. Nonetheless, the researchers have indicated that the development of such a new type of professionalism requires more support. In the next part, we will see that this concern laid the foundation for the search for a new type of professionalism of the individual and of the organizations in which all the existing qualifications (pre-school teacher, childcare mentor, children's healthcare worker, social worker) become integrated into a qualification framework.

The study brought forward some interesting data concerning the competencies of the management of an integrated Children's Centre. The evaluation study advocates a participatory leadership in which the decision-making processes are decentralised. Through the development of new management structures, new and clear function profiles have been created. In order to be able to work quickly, efficiently and in a more demand-oriented manner, according to the study, decisions can be made at the level of the teachers (Pascal, Bertram, 2005:177-178). This, too, will have its consequences and give rise to a new type of professionalism for the management. The management is, according to the researchers, a determining factor for the success of the integrated centres. Another important factor for the effects that an EEC has on parents and children is a well thought-out educational policy for personnel and management. In the EEC experiments, there were mostly staff members with a bachelor's diploma ('teachers'). Pascal and Bertram conclude that the EEC, with its well-trained and expert mentors and management, are excellent advocates for ECE and play a central role in the major processes of change in the English facilities for children (Pascal, Bertram, 2005: 184).

5.4.2.4. A spectacular expansion of the number of Children's Centres

As an answer to the outcome of the large evaluation study done by Pascal and Bertram – the objective of which was to search for a solution for the great amount of fragmentation in the sector – the government promised to invest 2 billion euros by 2006. The government – motivated by the success of the pilot projects – released funding for the development of a broad network of 'Children's Centres', that offer a wide range of services to children, families and neighbourhoods, and that are, in particular, set up in the poorer districts (Pascal, Bertram, 2005:174).

The investment in the Children's Centres (CC) has actually materialized. At the moment, there are 1500 working centres. By 2008, another 1000 should be added and, by 2010, a total of 3500 Children's Centres in England should be operational (Owens, Haynes, 2007).

5.4.3. In search of a new type of professionalism

The United Kingdom is illustrative of a policy that wants to implement a drastic change in the Children's Workforce – the professions for those who work with children. 'Workforce reform is seen as crucial to providing quality services for children and parents. At the centre of this reform process is a standards and target driven agenda to upgrade skill and professionalize the early years workforce' (Miller, 2006).

5.4.3.1. National Vocational Qualifications

15 years of experience with Recognising Earlier Acquired Competencies in the childcare sector

Since the end of the 1980s in the United Kingdom (Dorrance, 2007) there has been a system of 'National Vocational Qualifications', that was developed by the then government to acknowledge the skills and competencies that were acquired on the work floor. During the early 1990s, Sue Griffin was actively involved with the group that implemented the NVQ-system in the childcare sector. Griffin described the NVQs as follows: 'NVQs are competency-based qualifications, assessing candidates' performance, i.e. their ability to carry out the functions which make up their work – rather than just knowledge about their work' (Griffin, 1991: 344). In order to obtain an NVQ, the candidates must prove that they possess the necessary and proper competencies in actual work situations. During the implementation of the NVQ system in the early 1990s, there were – just as there are at the moment in Flanders with the implementation of the certificate of experience – heated discussions concerning the fact that the candidates were not being tested on their knowledge. Griffin then pointed out that knowledge certainly did play an important role in the NVQ procedure. 'But it is knowledge and understanding (i.e. attitudes) which underpin performance' (Griffin, 1991: 345). The qualification of an NVQ is awarded because of the competencies that the candidate has, independent of the manner in which he has obtained these competencies: through an official training course, by informal study, by experience, through personal growth or maturity or by a combination of all of these factors.

Until 1989, the United Kingdom did not have any diploma or qualification obligations for the staff members at facilities for young children (Hevey, Curtis, 1996: 212). The family day carers, who took on the greatest majority of the childcare places were, according to a study done by the Thomas Coram Institute, for the most part unqualified (Moss, Owen, Statham, Bull and Cameron, 1995: 5). In the Children's Act of 1989, a mentoring of the childcare staff members was recommended, but not required. For that reason, in 1989, the National Children's Bureau started a 'working with under Sevens' project. This project was commissioned to develop NVQ's for the 'Early Years.' More than 3000 teachers and members of management from all districts of the UK and from various types of facilities for young children were involved in the development of the standards for the NVQ's (Hevey, Curtis, 1996: 214).

The National Vocational Qualifications system was implemented in 1992 in the childcare sector and included two levels: level 2 (works under supervision) and level 3 (can work independently) (Oberhuemer, Ullich, 1997: 213). In 1994, two organizations that were involved in upgrading the professionalism in the professions that work with young children – the National Nursery Examination Board (NNEB) and the Early Years Award – founded a new organization: CACHE, the Council for Awards in Children's Care and Education (Cache, 2007). With the creation of CACHE as the 'awarding body', the NVQ system could be implemented in the childcare sector. CACHE remained responsible for the drafting of the standards of the NVQ's up through 2005 (Dorrance, 2007). Since 2005, the determination of the content of NVQ's has been entrusted to the Children's Workforce Development Council (CWDC), a subdivision of the Sector Skills Council, Skills for Care and Development. The role of CACHE is now limited to registering candidates, guaranteeing the quality of the qualification and supplying the certificates. The function of CACHE has been reduced to an 'awarding body' and other 'awarding bodies' have appeared on the market (Dorrance, 2007).

NVQ and VQ: Learning on the work floor

England has two systems for recognizing competencies: NVQ (National Vocational Qualification) and VQ (Vocational Qualification). A large number of people make use of this recognition system for qualifications. CACHE, as market leader, receives approximately 18,500 applications annually from candidates who want to go through the NVQ procedure, as opposed to 70,700 candidates who choose the VQ system (Dorrance, 2007).

The basic principles of the NVQ system are, thus far, still the same. The NVQ system is based on an assessment of acquired competencies. There is no written 'examination' administered, but the integrated knowledge, skills and competencies are tested via questioning, observation on the work floor and role play. The NVQ system is separate from formal training, but it is more than simply the recognition of previously acquired competencies. The candidate who requests an NVQ is admitted to a learning trajectory and the NVQ procedure gives the candidate the opportunity to upgrade the competencies. It takes no less than 15 months to complete the NVQ procedure for level 2 and another 15 months for level 3. During that period, the candidate prepares for the next step in his NVQ procedure. How the preparation occurs depends on the age of the candidate. The preparation for an NVQ is different for 16 to 19-year olds than for older candidates (Dorrance, 2007).

The young people (16 to 19-year olds) follow a kind of apprenticeship and are given an internship. During the internship, a coach prepares them for the various steps in the NVQ process. Right from the beginning of the introduction of the NVQ, there have been doubts as to whether or not the NVQ system is suitable for young people. 'Many experienced practitioners are sceptical of this method of training, believing maturity is an important quality for full-time work with children and that most 16-19-year-olds are better off on full-time education and training courses with limited work experience' (Hevey, Curtis, 1996: 218). According to Dorrance, the most motivated are in the early twenties to early thirties age group. They work in a childcare setting and it is the task of their employer to prepare them for the various steps in the NVQ procedure.

The administering of an assessment is expensive: 2000 British pounds or approximately 3000 euros. Thus far, 50% of all NVQ candidates have received financial support from the government. For young people with an apprenticeship, the entire amount was paid, the others received a stipend of 50% from the city council. This arrangement was recently changed; the government now feels that the employers must cover the costs. In the childcare sector, the employers are not, according to Dorrance, wealthy enough to do this. Dorrance expects, therefore, that there will be problems in the future.

A 'Vocational Qualification' takes two years and half of the time is spent doing the internship; the other half consists of course work. The assessment occurs via a written examination and not through observation on the work floor. It is a 'pass or fail' system by which the candidate is either successful or not. There are no grades issued. It costs the assessor 40 hours per candidate to make the assessment.

Weaknesses in the system

Based on his years of experience, the director of CACHE, Richard Dorrance, has formulated two weaknesses in both the NVQ and the VQ systems. Research has shown that it is extremely difficult to guarantee the quality of the assessments. An assessment is, after all, difficult to standardize. It turns out that the assessors are strongly inclined to impose their own vision on the interpretation of the assessment. Richard Dorrance summarized it as follows: 'Assessment is not a science' (Dorrance, 2007).

Nevertheless, high standards have been set for the assessment centres in England. Each centre must have its assessors supervised both internally and externally.

A second problem is that the candidates who apply for an NVQ or a VQ have a long wait – due to the shortage of assessors – before they can start the procedure. In order to become an assessor, a 6 to 7 month training course is necessary and a diploma in childcare is also required.[4]

5.4.3.2. Building a world-class workforce for children

Upgrading qualifications

In the United Kingdom, there are many ways to gain access to an occupation in ECE: 'In England (and the whole of the UK) there is a confusing variation in the type and level of training required for working with young children' (Miller, 2006: 3). England is, as is Flanders, confronted with the problem that a large number of the childcare workers is not qualified. It appears that 40% of the childcare workers have not even achieved the level 2, a basic level of training according to the NVQ system. Only 12% seems to be qualified at level 6 (bachelor). The British government has been convinced by the EPPE study (Sylva et al, 2004) that the quality of the provisions is clearly linked to the training level of the staff members and that a coherent policy must be implemented to upgrade the qualifications of the childcare workers: 'Workforce reform is therefore seen as crucial to providing quality services for children and parents' (H.M. Treasure, 2004). On April 1 2005, the British government launched a consultation document: 'The Children's Work Strategy: a strategy to build a world class workforce for children and young people.'

---

4   A candidate assessor must achieve level 4 in assessment and he/she must also achieve level 3 in 'Childcare'.

(HM Government, 2005). In this 'Children's Workforce Strategy', the government chooses to have a 'world-class workforce' which can provide the children with the best possible opportunities, which can reduce the inequality in chances between the under-privileged and other children and which can allow the sector to better anticipate new needs.

A Common Core for all professions with young children

For this reason, the 'Children's Workforce Strategy' will have developed an integrated qualification framework for the childcare professions by 2015. An important new organ that is to support and mentor this process is the 'Children's Workforce Development Council'. For this purpose, within the CWDC, the Children's Workforce Network was established with representatives from a wide range of professional groups which work with children.

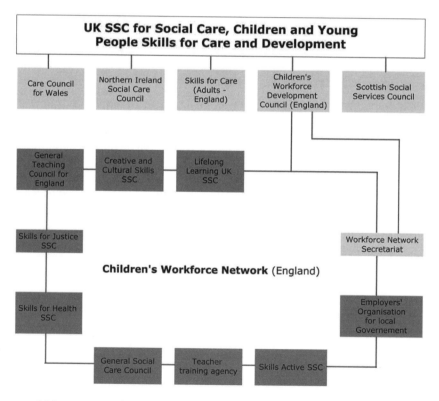

www.everychildmatters.gov.uk

As director of the National Children's Bureau, Paul Ennals was appointed chairman of the Children's Workforce Network, an influential organization for everyone in England who works with children. In an interview, Ennals stated that this network was attempting to get all of the professional organizations to the table to shape the new 'Children's Workforce'. Ennals' strategy consisted of bringing representatives of family day carers, childcare workers, parents, teachers, pediatric social workers and healthcare workers together to think about and work on collective values in working with children (Ennals, 2007). The CWN seeks to develop a 'common core', a collective package of competencies, skills and knowledge for all staff members working with children. 'The Common Core of Skills and Knowledge for the Children's Workforce sets out the basic skills and knowledge needed by people (including volunteers) whose work brings them into regular contact with children, young people and families. It will enable multi-disciplinary teams to work together more effectively in the interests of the child' (Every Child Matters, 2006).

A differentiation is made among six domains that are important for all professional groups working with children: effective communication and involvement with children; knowledge of child development; the ability to realize the safety and welfare of children; the ability to guide the transitions that children make throughout their lives in a sympathetic manner; the ability to work in a multifunctional service and the ability to process information and share it with others.

It is the intention of the CWN that, within the foreseeable future, everyone who works with children and their families will have mastered the basic competency level in these six 'Common Core' areas. In the future, this 'Common Core' will form the basis for all training programmes that are organized by educational and retraining organizations. By linking the professional profiles with each other, there will be more horizontal mobility and the profession will become more attractive. In this way, the CWN hopes, in the future, to be able to attract the necessary manpower. Because of the spectacular expansion of – among other things – the Children's Centres, there is a danger of a labour market shortage.

Integrated qualification framework

According to the CWN, the Children's Workforce needs an 'overarching framework' and, with this goal in mind, a well-developed, integrated qualification framework.

The wide variety of possibilities for access to professions in childcare will remain in place for the time being, but will be placed within an 'Integrated Qualifications Framework,' depending upon the qualifications or school results that have been achieved. [5]

Qualifications can cross boundaries a rough guide to comparing qualifications in the UK and Ireland May 2005		
Main stages of education/employment	**England, Wales & Northern Ireland National Qualifications Framework** www.qca.org.uk/qualifications www.accac.org.uk www.qca.org.uk/openquals www.ccea.org.uk	**England, Wales and Northern Ireland framework for higher education qualifications: FHEQ** www.qaa.ac.uk/adacemicinfrastructure/fheq
Qualifications can be taken at any age in order to continue or return to education or training	**Entry level** Entry level certificate (NQf)	
Secondary education Initial entry into employment or further education	**Level 1** NVQ Level 1 Level 1 Certificate GCSEs at grade D-G	
Continuation of Secondary education Progression to skilled employment	**Level 2** NVQ Level 2 Level 2 Certificate Level 2 Diploma GCSEs at grade A*-C	
Completion of secondary education Entry to higher education Qualified/Skilled worker	**Level 3** NVQ Level 3 A* Levels Level 3 Certificate Level 3 Diploma	
Specialised education and training	**Level 4** NVQs Level 4 Certificate Level 4 Diploma	**Level C** Certificates of Higher Education
Entry to professional graduate employment Intermediate/Higher education Advanced skills training	**Level 5** NVQs Level 5 Certificate Level 5 Diploma Higher National Diploma	**Level I** Ordinary Bachelor's degree Foundation Degrees Diplomas of higher education other higher diplomas
	Level 6 (EYPS) NVQs Level 6 Certificate Level 6 Diploma	**Level H** Bachelor's degrees with honours Graduate certificates and diplomas
Professional or postgraduate education or employment	**Level 7 (NPQICL)** NVQs Level 7 Diploma Level 7 Fellowship Level 7 Advanced Professional Certificate	**Level M** Master's degree postgraduate diplomas postgraduate certificates
	Level 8 Highly specialist Diploma from a professional body	**Level D** Doctoral degree

---

5   The Integrated Qualification Framework in England is in conformity with the European Qualification Framework.

The IQF system has 8 levels. The official organ, the Children's Workforce Development Council (CWDC), determines the level at which someone can start in the childcare sector, depending on the course of training and VQs that the person has taken and the competencies achieved that have been determined via an assessment (NVQs). Just as in the European Qualification Framework, a learning path is also central to this IQF system, with the intention of upgrading the competencies over time and stimulating vertical mobility in the 'Children's Workforce'. This learning path gives the staff member the possibility to achieve a higher competency or training level via, if necessary, such assessment procedures as NVQs or VQs or via training modules in Adult Education. It is essential in this system that they are supported by an educational and competency policy that is carried out by the facilities and supported by government. In concluding this chapter on IQF, we will list the advantages of this system.

The IQF offers – just as the European Qualification Framework – a clear course of training and employment opportunities for the future, so that childcare workers know where they can work with which qualifications and which achieved competencies.

It simplifies the formal recognition of achieved knowledge and experience so that staff members can use this in building their careers.

It clarifies how an employee can gain access to higher training courses and qualifications.

It stimulates life-long learning and is a means for upgrading the competency of the entire sector that, on the one hand, is based on the recognition of earlier acquired competencies and, on the other hand, also recognizes the formal training that has been done.

For the employer, this IQF offers a clear and unambiguous framework for the hiring of personnel. It gives the employers a handle for an efficient personnel policy.

5.4.3.3. The Early Years Professional

The objectives of the British government to design a 'world-class workforce for children' have also led to a discussion on which type of training is necessary at the bachelor and master's levels. 'The Government's national consultation on the future of the children's workforce highlighted the need to develop a group of people able to take on a new lead professional role' (DfES, 2005).

The EPPE studies (Sylva, et al, 2004) have shown that it was, in particular, the presence of teachers (comparable to our kindergarten teachers) that made the difference in the children's chances for development. However, teachers are a rare sight in the childcare sector and the majority of the staff members in the provisions for young children were unqualified employees (Miller, 2006:3). For this reason, the British Government went in search of a 'graduate equivalent' (Broadhead, 2007: 05 18), an alternative for the bachelor's degree that could be attained by a part of the low-schooled personnel in the sector. Thus, after consultation with the sector, the 'Early Years Professional' was created.

The CWDC wants to start from the existing training trajectories and build a number of extra modules (based on the Common Core) into the various training courses. At the same time, the CWDC wants to create an adapted course of training that will make it possible to offer the lower level employees the opportunity to become Early Years Professionals (CWDC, 2006) and, thus, to advance to more qualified jobs. The competency model goes up to level 3 and the CWS wants to raise this to level 6. The policy structures for implementing this objective are available in England; there are, after all, a sufficient number of assessors and organisations (including CACHE) that could take on this ambitious project.

The EYP is, according to Broadhead (2007; 04 24): 'a status, not a diploma'. This status can be attained via various paths. The teachers who already have a master's degree can apply for the EYP status, but have to complete a validation process. At the moment, EYP candidates have to achieve graduate status before they can complete EYP status, although CWDC are looking to open up undergraduates routes (Miller, 2007).

Bertram and Pascal advocate a training course that creates 'reflective practitioners' and which integrates theory and practice. 'The trainings that we have until now in the ECEC sector in the UK have been vocationally based, they adopted a competency approach, they listed a series of competencies and then went out to the workplace and obtained evidence that they saw the competencies in action. But this approach is very practical and skills based, and what we need is a deeper reflective analytical approach which doesn't lend itself well to the competency approach. The English teacher training has that more reflective approach. The evidence of the EPPE research was saying that a training that was integrating practice and theory seemed to have a positive impact on the way practitioners understood the children's development and was able to refine the actions of the practitioners' (Pascal, 2007: 03 00). Pascal does not want to go as far as promoting the teacher training course as the only training in the provisions for young children because, she feels, this training course is also not optimal for the Childcare sector. She points out that the 'reflective approach' has been imbedded in the teacher-training course since the 1970s (Pascal, 2007: 04 25). Bertram is also of the opinion that this merging of theory and practice within the training course leading to the EYP status is of essential importance for the quality of the provisions (Bertram, 2007: 03 30).

According to Pascal, the greatest challenge for the British Government and for the Children's Workforce Network lies in bringing that large group of staff members who have attained their qualifications via the 'competency-based model' up to the higher bachelor's level. The CWN must raise the low-qualified (NVQ and VQ level 1 and 2) 'children's workforce' to a graduate level (bachelor's or master's – level 4 or level 6). Pascal and Bertram fear that this will again occur via this 'competency-based approach' (NVQ and VQs) and much less via the integrated theory-practice approach that can be found in the teacher training courses. A training for reflective practitioner would, after all, require a longer training time and, consequently, also be more expensive. Pascal and Bertram doubt, moreover, that the great majority of these low-qualified childcare staff members would be able to handle this type of training course (Pascal, 2007: 05 00).

Pascal, Bertram (2007) and also Broadhead (2007) are critical of extending this competency model to 'graduate levels'. The qualification at level 6 should, according to Pascal, start from a more analytical and reflective framework; it should be based on the combination of theory and practice that can be found in the teacher training courses. The 'best practice' in the provisions for young children in England was, according to Bertram and Pascal, to be found in the nursery schools where kindergarten teachers worked. They had received, in their basic training, that rich mixture of theory and practice, just as elementary and secondary school teachers did. Pascal does not find the theory and reflection on the practice in these 'common core competencies.'
Not everyone, however, believes that the teacher training (primary school teacher) is suitable. 'There have, however, been concerns that such teachers are not necessarily trained to work with the youngest children and early years teacher education courses do not cover the birth to three age range. Approximately 20,000 settings in the private and voluntary sector do not employ a teacher' (Miller, 2006).

The Early Years Sector-Endorsed Foundation Degrees

Miller believes, on the other hand, in the opportunities offered by the Early Years endorsed Foundation Degrees. In 2001, a new career path was opened up for early years practitioners that would lead to the role of Senior Practitioner. This can be obtained by taking an Early Years Sector-Endorsed Foundation Degree (EYSEFD). Foundation Degrees are vocational qualifications that have been developed in order to integrate an academic course of study with in-house training. Sector-endorsed Foundation Degrees are recognized by representatives of a well-determined professional sector and have been developed by the employers to create precisely those workers that they need. The government has recorded – in a 'Statement of Requirements' – precisely what employers expect from an experienced staff member (Senior Practitioner). This Foundation Degree has created a new level of professional practice that, moreover, offers the possibility to go on to achieve a bachelor's level ('a graduate status or Qualified Teacher Status') by means of on-the-job training and part-time course work.

The EYSEFD focuses on practitioners who work with children from birth to the age of 8, who possess the necessary skills and experience, but whose qualification level is relatively low. EYSEFD gives experienced staff members the possibility to combine work and study and gives thus far unprecedented opportunities in vertical mobility.

Miller (2006) believes that – in spite of the 'technical approach' typical of the competency model – it is possible to organize training courses within the regulatory framework that would create 'Reflective Early Years Professionals'. The Early Years Foundation Degree at the Open University is such a training course that develops a reflective practitioner, one who is inspired by the four levels of activities developed by Oberhuemer (2005), (interacting with the children, centre management and leadership, partnership with parents and professional knowledge base). 'It builds on the notion of 'reflective practice', introduced to students in the knowledge-based courses, to describe a way of approaching their work that involves questioning why and how they do something while they are actually doing it' (Cable, Goodliff, Miller, 2007: 6). The Open University uses, in this training course, the 'Reflective Practice Cycle' or RPC method. The four levels of the RPC method are: 'thinking about practice, exploring practice, reflecting on practice and documenting evidence' (Cable, Goodliff, Miller, 2007: 7). They also work with a 'Three Layer Model of Practice', that enables students to visualise the moving interactions between their day-to-day practice and how their knowledge, values and beliefs influence the way in which they work with children and support their understanding of the process of reflection (Cable, Goodliff, Miller, 2007: 7).

The Open University has checked to see if this method has an effect on the behavior of the students. The students find the reflecting on their own practice difficult but, towards the end of their studies, when the students must write papers on the changes they have instigated in their work, it appears that: 'They were able to reflect on the challenges to their thinking and to provide some powerful examples of the impact on their practice' (Cable, Goodliff, Miller, 2007:13).

The opponents of the Early Years Professional feel, on the one hand, that the current climate does, indeed, offer possibilities, but they are also cautious about the technical interpretation of professionalism that is connected to the current thinking about competency. 'The state-driven professionalism agenda as set out in recent government policy documents, presents an attractive and seductive opportunity to raise the status and prestige of ECEC' (Osgood, 2006b: 9).

'England provides a clear example of the early years worker as a technician in the case of its childcare workforce' (Moss, 2006: 35). These technicians may have very different levels of skills and qualifications. 'Their role is to apply a defined set of technologies through regulated processes to produce pre-specified and measurable outcomes.' The government gives a precise description of what employees in the provisions for young children can achieve and has laid this down in a detailed curriculum and in a set of 60 objectives. According to Moss, this will encourage conformity within the sector (Moss, 2006: 36).

Alongside of this, a career structure should be developed. Young people with a lower qualification (level 1, 2 or 3) must have the opportunity to rise to a higher level 6: the 'Early Years Professional'. The purpose of the 'transformation fund' is, in the first instance, to make this possible for the private and volunteer sector. However, according to Broadhead, few make use of the opportunities that are offered via this fund. The private sector does not, after all, want to pay its staff who want to follow the courses or take part in the assessment a higher salary, so that the motivation among the staff members to take on a training course or an NVQ disappears. Miller (2006) believes that it is possible – in spite of the 'technical approach' inherent in the competency model – to organize training courses within the regulatory framework that would train a 'Reflective Early Years Professional'. Bertram and Pascal also believe that the quality of the EYP is strongly dependent upon who grants the status.

The researchers at the Thomas Coram Institute (University of London) (Moss, Petrie, 2002: 141; Cameron, 2004; 2006; Moss, 2006) therefore advocate a review of the existing training courses; 'a reconceptualisation of the workforce' (Cameron, 2004: 11). 'The childcare worker attempts to become a co-creator, rather than merely a transmitter of knowledge.' The researchers would like to see a new profession and a new training course be developed on the Danish model: 'the social pedagogue'. 'The function of the pedagogue is to help children to establish, re-establish or maintain identity, solidarity and meaning: to engage with and commit to other people (solidarity); and to help them to be able to interpret the social culture (meaning)' (Cameron, 2004: 12). 'For the pedagogue, learning, care and upbringing are indivisible activities; these are not distinct fields that must somehow be joined up, but interconnected facets of life that cannot be envisaged separately' (Moss, 2006: 32)[6]. A number of important actors within the Children's Development Workforce Council and the Children's Workforce Network (Miller, 2006; Ennals, 2007; Haynes, 2007; Dorrance, 2007) do not believe in the feasibility of creating a new profession of 'pedagogue'. According to Ennals, the chairman of the Children's Workforce Network, it is taboo for the existing professional groups (health workers, teachers, social workers,...) to create a new profession of social 'pedagogue'. For these reasons, the Children's Workforce Development Council has chosen the 'Early Years Professional role.' Pascal (2007: 17 00) sees no point in introducing a new profession of 'pedagogue'; she feels that the strong points in the English system must be further developed and that is the 'reflective approach' in the teacher training course. In England, there is no tradition in pedagogy; it is a word that does not even exist in English. By introducing the 'pedagogue' in the provisions, there is a danger that the ties to the educational system will be severed. Since 1998, 'early childhood education' has been a part of the educational system and, according to Pascal, so must it remain.

The discussion has, however, not been closed; in a recently published issue of the journal 'Issues in the Early Years' (2006, nr.1) and during an international conference organized by the Thomas Coram Institute of the University of London in December 2006, Cameron, Moss and Petri persevered in their plea for a new training course for 'pedagogue.' In an interview, Moss states that he is especially disappointed about the fact that there has been no in-depth discussion on the type of professional that Early Childhood Education in England needs. (Moss, 2007). He does see that there is major interest for the social

---

6   This interpretation of professionalism is closely linked to that of the social pedagogue (*sociaal agogisch werker*) in The Netherlands, Flanders or Germany.

pedagogue in the residential facilities, but fears that the 'pedagogue' in the future will only be introduced into this sector and not in Early Childhood Education (Moss, 2007).

5.4.4. Conclusion

The changes in the sector of provisions for young children in England are, for several reasons, interesting for other European countries that find themselves in the midst of a professionalization process. In many European countries, just as in England, the great majority of the personnel are low-qualified (OECD, 2006). Many countries have a large number of places in areas of the sector where no qualification requirements have been set: this is especially the case with childminders or family day carers and also in commercial daycare centres. Alongside of this, we have seen that – for the past 15 years – the English have used a competency-based system in the childcare sector. In most the countries in continental Europe, this system has only been in place for the past few years and does not yet have a vision on the manner in which it must occur (Peeters, 2005). The English experience is of importance for the manner in which one must deal with the recognition of earlier acquired competencies. The NVQ approach differs fundamentally from the approach in some EU member states, for example Flanders. In these countries, the earlier acquired competencies system is seen as an assessment to award a qualification to the candidate on the basis of competencies that are seen to have been previously acquired and does not aim to upgrade the competencies. In England, it is certainly the intention of the NVQ system to upgrade the competencies. This occurs by making an assessment over a longer period of time, so that the candidate can prepare himself and be included in a course of study.

Another point of interest concerns the quality of the assessors who administer the NVQs. The high quality requirements that England sets for its assessors is in sharp contrast to the reality in many European countries. In Flanders, for example, the EVC assessment procedures for staff members in pre-school childcare (VIVO, 2006) used assessors who had taken a two-day training course. For these assessors, there were no provisions made for supervision and they were not required to have had any experience in childcare. The English experience has already made it abundantly clear that it is of crucial importance for the reliability of the assessments that the assessors receive an appropriate training in administering assessments – and in childcare.

In England, the NVQ-VQ system has been well developed, with well-trained assessors and official 'councils' which monitor and regulate the system. Moreover, the system is continually being judged on its strengths and weaknesses by numerous researchers.

Various researchers (Osgood, 2006b; Moss, 2006, Bertram & Pascal, 2007; Broadhead, 2007) have expressed a fundamental criticism of the NVQ-VQ system. In most of the European countries, the competency model that is slowly making its entrance into the childcare and other sectors (education and welfare) has hardly been criticized at all. In England, this system of VQs and NVQs, that has been in practice for some time and has been greatly expanded, has been fundamentally questioned by various authors. As far as these authors are concerned, the competency-based model stands for a technical interpretation of professionalism, which is in sharp contrast to the 'reflective practitioner' that is requested at international forums (Moss, Petri, 2002; OECD, 2006; Bertram & Pascal, 2007; Broadhead, 2007). Moss goes even further by arguing that these ideas about competency – by determining the competencies and outcomes – would encourage conformism within the sector (Moss, 2006). The competency model would curb innovation within the childcare sector and result in uninspired uniformity.

The Integrated Qualifications Framework refers to a technical interpretation of professionalism, but we agree with Miller (2006) that this framework offers opportunities to upgrade the professionalism of low-qualified staff members. In England – just as in many other European countries – it is necessary to upgrade the many childcare staff members with a lower qualification via a course of study to a higher qualification. It is probable that the European Qualification Framework, that will be implemented in time, will play an important role in this process. It is the intention of the EQF to integrate courses of study, diplomas and EVC's so that childcare workers know where they can go with which qualifications and which attained competencies.

Finally, the conclusions drawn by Pascal and Bertram (2005) from the evaluation of the Early Excellence Centres pilot projects are important for the type of professionalism that we will need in the near future. Their study proves the importance of such training for leadership. The absorbing discussion that is being carried on within the English research world on the interpretation of a training course at the bachelor and master's degree levels for leaderhip, can be an inspiration for all European countries.

5.5. France: a social worker/educator for the youngest children and their parents

5.5.1. Methods followed

This section on the evolution of the interpretation of professionalism in France is inspired by a literature study, by an intensive collaboration starting in 1991 on projects of the European Social Fund with French partners: the federation of parent crèches, ACEPP (Association Collectifs Enfant Parents Professionnels) in Paris and the training college for *éducateur jeunes enfants* and *auxiliaires de puériculture*, Ecole Santé Social Sud Est (ESSSE) in Lyon, and on interviews with one of the main figures, Myriam Mony, director of ESSSE.

The collaboration with ESSE has been fairly intensive since 1998: an annual workship for students was organized by VBJK staff members and twice a year, on average, we have given lectures, workshops and lessons on the subjects of ethnic and gender diversity for students and graduates of the training college in Lyon. This contact with students and graduates, has awakened our interest in the training course *éducateur jeunes enfants* (EJE).

For more then 15 years we have taken part in many conferences for EJE. These conferences have given us the chance to form a picture of the interpretation of professionalism for the educator of young children (EJE) in France.

We also made a study trip to the *Centre de Recherche sur la Formation* (Art et Métier, Paris), where we studied the literature on professionalism in the social pedagogical professions that had been published by this *Centre de Recherche sur la Formation* (Paul, 2004; Barbier, 2005; Sorel, Wittorski, 2005; Barbier, Bourgeois, de Villers, Kaddouri, 2006).

5.5.2. Childcare in France

France and Belgium occupy a unique position within the European Union because both Member States have developed a system of *école maternelle*, or preschool, that is free for the parents and where all children can be placed from a very young age (OECD, 2006: 325). Starting in the 1960s, both countries have also succeeded in achieving a large number of subsidized places in childcare for children in the 0-3 age group (Moss, 1988; 1996).

The French system of childcare has a strongly-developed network of family day carers: the *assistentes maternelles* who are generally affiliated with a *crèche familiale* (service for family day carers), and the *garde à domicile* (in-home care givers). Within the system of group childcare, there are also *crèches collectives* (subsidized childcare centres), *haltes garderies* (occassional childcare) and *crèches parentales* (small associative crèches run by parents) (OECD, 2006: 327).

Seventy-five percent of the childcare staff must have a diploma of *puéricultrice* (nurse), *éducateur jeunes enfants* or *auxilaire de puériculture* (childcare worker at secondary level); the other, non-qualified employees must be supervised on the work floor. For *école maternelle*, a university diploma of *professeurs des écoles* is required, but this *diplôme d'état* has the disadvantage that it is not specifically focused on early childhood education: 'Certificaton in early childhood studies and pedagogy can be weak' (OECD, 2006: 332).

From the perspective of professionalization, there are – alongside of the differences – also a number of similarities between France and Belgium (Peeters, 2007:37).

The French system of childcare has, for example – just as the Belgium system – a strong medical-hygienic history (Mony, 1994: 17; Humblet, 1998; Vandenbroeck, 2004; Cadart, 2006: 13).

The content of the French training course *auxiliare de puériculture* displays great similarities to the training course *Kinderzorg* [Childcare] and both courses are organized at the level of Secondary Professional Education (Oberhuemer, Ulich, 1997: 86).

The training course *éducateur jeunes enfants* has, since its conception in 1973, provided a strong impulse to the professionalization of the services for young children in a direction that is more oriented towards social pedagogy. Starting in 2005, it has become a training course at the Bachelor level (Mony, 2002:73). In this chapter, we will study the evolution within this training course and the impact that it has had on a new interpretation of professionalism within the French system of childcare. We also question the extent to which this course provides an answer to what the Anglo-Saxon-inspired literature calls the 'reflective practitioner' or 'the worker researcher'. In conclusion, we study whether or not the diversity of training courses and the vertical and horizontal mobility that is inherent in the French system of qualifications can be an inspiration for other European countries.

5.5.3. The evolution of professionalism in the professions dealing with young children

5.5.3.1. The rise of various forms of professionalism

Since the beginning of the twentieth century, the process of professionalization in the French childcare system has been characterized by the fact that professionals with various job descriptions – and sometimes even opposing visions of the work involved – have entered the sector. The *infirmières puéricultrices* (pediatric nurses) and the *auxiliaires de puériculture* (assistant to the pediatric nurse), who received an official statute in 1947 and 1971, respectively, were the first crop of professionals in childcare. The interpretation of professionalism for these professions was based on the notion of care: *une logique de soin pour jeunes enfants* (Mony, 2002: 76; Verba, 2005: 45). The similarity with the situation in Belgium is striking (Mony, 1994: 17)[7]. The management in the childcare sector in Belgium consisted, during that time, also exclusively of nurses and the *auxiliaire en puériculture* can be compared with the Belgian training course *Kinderverzorging* [Childcare] (Mony, 1994:19). The training courses *infirmières puéricultrices* and *auxilaires de puériculture* were originally charged with the task of reducing infant mortality and placed, therefore, the emphasis on the medical-hygienic aspects. Educational content was hardly an issue at all (Humblet, 1998; Vandenbroeck, 2004; Mony, 2006: 21).

The *assistentes maternelles* (family day carers) subscribe to the logic of individual childcare. In 1977, the French family day carers were provided with a statute and, starting in 1992, a 60-hour preliminary training course has been required (Mony, 2002:76).

Since the beginning of the twentieth century, there has also been a training course for *jardinières d'enfants*. The first course was set up in 1907 by Mademoiselle Gahery and, in the second half of the twentieth century, the *jardins d'enfants* organized themselves into a federation. By 1935, there were 10 private training institutes that had organized the training of *jardinière d'enfants* (Chebboldaeff, 2006: 22). The exclusively female students, in this initial period, came from the higher social economic milieus and most of them were employed in their profession for only a short period of time before they themselves became mothers and stayed home to raise their own children (Réty, in Verba, 2006: 69). These *Kindergartens* were inspired by the pedagogy of Fröbel and Pestalozzi. '*Les jardins d'enfants considèrent l'éducation non comme un dressage, mais plutôt*

---

7 In Belgium, as well, we see that it is first the nurses who were given a place in the childcare sector and, from 1970, the diploma *Kinderverzorging* [Childcare] was mandatory.

comme un accompagnement; l'enfant, non comme un petit sauvage dangereux qu'il faut discipliner par la force, mais comme un être déjà humain dont il convient seulement de guider les premières pas' (Verba, 2006: 56). The training centres for *jardinière d'enfants* were not official schools, but were affiliated with the private Catholic education system. The graduates found work primarily in the *écoles maternelles* and in the *haltes garderies* (Mony, 2007: 6.00). In 1967, the training centres established a national organization with the intention of creating a *diplôme d'état* from the *jardinière d'enfant*. Since, in 1965, half of all *jardinières d'enfants* were employed in the *écoles maternelles* (Verba, 2006: 72), the organization of training courses attempted to gain recognition by the Ministry *Education Nationale*, but this failed. '*Sans doute la vieille querelle entre enseignement laïc et l'enseignement privé, assimilé à l'enseignement religieux, a faussé les négociations.*' (Chebboldaef, 2006: 23). The Debré law from the end of the 1950s determined that pre-school (*école maternelle*) and primary school (*école primaire*) teachers should have the same training. For the education unions – and also for many inspectors of public education – it was, therefore, a taboo subject that teachers in the *écoles maternelles* would receive a special training course for working with toddlers such as the *jardinières d'enfant* were receiving.

5.5.3.2. The Educateur Jeunes Enfants: working towards a socio-pedagogical interpretation of professionalism

After the refusal from *Education Nationale*, the national organization of educational institutes commenced negotiations with the *Ministère de Santé Publique*, which issued the *diplômes d'état* for social workers and specialized educators. A few years later, in 1973, the negotiations were successfully completed and a new training course, *éducateur jeunes enfants* was created. The duration of the training for EJE was set at two years, while the training course for social worker and specialized educator was three years. '*Le diplôme d'Etat d'Educateurs de Jeunes Enfants en 1973 ouvre des perspectives plus modernes, donne la possibilité aux hommes d'entrer dans le monde très féminisé de la petite enfance, enfin il apporte aux centres des subventions qui vont rendre les études gratuites et donc s'ouvrir à des étudiants, qui avant ça, ne pouvaient pas envisager cette formation.*' (Chebboldaef, 2006: 23). Just as with the other social training courses, a preliminary selection is mandatory and the setting of diploma requirements (a *baccalauréat* or an equivalent diploma such as *auxiliaire de puériculture*) is strongly recommended. The *Educateur Jeunes Enfants* was, with this recognition as a *diplôme d'état*, admitted into the social professions, and this had far-reaching consequences: in 1965, half of the *jardinières d'enfants* were employed in the teaching professions; in 2005, nearly all of the EJE graduates were employed in the social sector (Verba, 2006: 72).

In the tradition of the *jardinières d'enfants*, the Federation of EJE's continues to believe in the construction of the competent child: '*L'EJE doit considèrer l' enfant comme une personne compétente et capable de communication*' (Grenel, 2000: 7). The task of the *éducateur jeunes enfants* was described by the Federation of EJE as follows: '*Accompagner l'enfant c'est créer les conditions qui vont à l'enfant permettre de se faire œuvre de lui même, c'est aménager l'espace et le temps, c'est être porteur des règles en leur donnant du sens, être sécurisant, offrir une présence sûre et solide sur la quelle l'enfant pourra toujours compter.*' (FNEJE, 2000).

Mony (2006) and Verba (2006) point out the important evolution that the training course for *éducateur jeunes enfants* has undergone since 1973. A number of social changes – including the influx of a large number of young mothers into the labor market – and the increasing diversity within families, have given rise to new types of childcare which require a different kind of professionalism (Doucet-Dahlgren, 2004: 70). Therefore, for the past few years, a great deal of attention has been paid in the courses to working with ethnic minority families, blended families, divorced and single parents and same-sex parents. '*Cette évolution a marqué le passage fondamental de la prise en charge de l'enfant considéré de manière isolée à une prise en charge de l'enfant pensée en lien permanent avec ses référents familiaux, son contexte social et culturel. Cette conception permet une continuité éducative dans la discontinuité des lieux de vie de l'enfant (famille, crèche) du fait des décalages entre les modèles éducatifs à l'œuvre entre famille et structure d'accueil.*' (Mony, 2006: 25).

In the early 1990s, the French sociologist Daniël Verba laid the foundation for a 'social pedagogy' training course of 2½ years that stands midway between a training for child carer and one for social worker (Meunier, Chétoui, 2002: 8). Working with parents is going to be central in the interpretation of professionalism of the EJE. '*L'intervention de l'EJE trouve sa place aujourd'hui au sein de deux systèmes: celui de la famille et celui du social, c'est-à-dire la prise en compte de l'environnement et ses complexités.*' (Verba, 2006: 134-135). This means that the individuality of each child and his specific family and cultural bonds are acknowledged and, at the same time, a coherent educational plan will be realized for all children and their parents. '*La rencontre avec la problématique de la diversité devient inhé-*

rente à la pratique professionnelle et la nécessité de la travailler en formation est un impératif.'
(Mony, 2006:27). The EJE is a social worker who operates on the boundary of social intervention and prevention. Working with parents is seen as an essential part of working with
children. This new interpretation of the task of the EJE can be retraced to the reform of
the training course in 1993, which expanded the duration of the course to two-and-a-half
years. EJE became a training course that prepared the student to work with children from
0 to 7 years old, outside of school: in daycare centres, *haltes garderies* (occasional care), toy
libraries and institutions for children with special needs.

After 1993, the EJE begins to include an increasing number of management functions,
particularly in parent crèches, the services for family day carers and in the *haltes garderies*.
In the *crèches collectives*, the *puéricultrices*/nurses continue to take on the management
functions. (Gaberan, 2000: 6). That would not change until the decree *Petite enfance* of
August 1 2000 that gives the EJE with five years' experience access to a management function in daycare centres with fewer than 40 children (art. 180-15b). It appears, from a
study by Meunier and Chétoui (2002: 135) that the EJEs, however, feel that they are in-
sufficiently well prepared for a management function. Those EJEs who were questioned
would also like to be better prepared to mentor less-qualified staff members. In reality,
many EJE's must coach a team of childcare workers or family day carers. For that reason,
they have asked that *l'encadrement des professionnels* be included in the basic training
course (Meunier en Chétoui: 2002: 101).

According to Verba, the history of the EJE was determined by two arguments that were
among the determining factors for the interpretation of professionalism (Verba, 2005:48).
The first one was thrashed out with teachers of the *école maternelle*. The professionalism
of the EJE is based on a strong pedagogic interpretation which, however, is not realized
via instruction or via the handing down of academic knowledge. The professionalism
of the EJE places the accent on the welcoming reception and the relationship with the
children and their parents and on the spontaneous possibilities of the child. In this area,
the professionalism of the EJE dovetails with the 'competent child' of the North-Italian
(Rinaldi, 2005) and Scandinavian pedagogy (Brembeck, et al, 2004). The joys of spontaneous learning have precedent over an instructional approach: *l'aspect disciplinaire des
apprentissages*. There is a great contrast with the teacher at the *école maternelle*: she interprets professionalism as the assessment of the children's achievements according to a set
standard (for example, you must learn to read at the age of…).

The other professional group with whom the EJE has done battle is the *puéricultrices*
(pediatric nurses) because the EJEs reject the paramedical approach to young children

and also because the *puéricultrices* still fulfil most of the management functions in the 'crèches collectives'.

Each profession needs, according to Verda, enemies in order to construct its own professional identity. The EJEs have created their professional identity by rebelling against the school and medical science and they have found their inspiration in educational rebels who were extremely attached to values of social justice, such as Françoise Dolto, Donald Winnicot, Maria Montessori and Célestin Freinet (Verba, 2005: 48).

5.5.4. Recent evolutions in the training course for EJE

5.5.4.1. Analyse de pratiques

The Parisian *Centre du Recherche sur la Formation,* which included Jean-Marie Barbier and Richard Wittorski (chapter 3), has developed the method of the *analyse de pratiques,* for the social and educational professions, the objective of which is to reflect on the practice from a theoretical framework (Wittorski, 2005; Barbier, 2006). As far as Barbier is concerned, professionalization within a training course is a finite process of transformation of competencies, in relation to a process of transformation of activities. By analyzing the practical experiences of the students – first on an individual basis and later in group form – this professionalization process is steered and supported (Meunier, 2004: 118). This *analyse de pratiques,* is also given an important place in the development of professionalism within the EJE training course (Fablet, ed. 2004). '*Ces nouvelles formes de formation, telles que les temps d'analyse de la pratique ont comme objectifs non seulement l'acquisition de savoirs mais aussi la production de savoirs liée aux situations de travail et le développement de compétences pour l'apprenant'* (Meunier, 2004: 126). In the first year, via this analysis of intership experiences, the foundation is laid for a personal track towards professionalism. In the second and third years, the situations that the student interns had experienced that did not work well in human and/or organizational areas are discussed in the group. Using this approach, Meunier (2004: 127) seeks to develop new competencies among the students, so that it then becomes possible for them – later, as professionals – to anticipate unforeseen pedagogic situations. According to Didier Favre,[8] the *analyse de pratiques* is a method the intention of which is to elicit more

---

8   In the 1990s, Didier Favre was employed in ACEPP, the federation of crèches parentales. During that time, Myriam Mony was responsible within the ACEPP for the education department and Mony and Favre started an experiment concerned with learning on the work floor. (Cadart, 2006: 31). The analysis of practical situations played an important role in this 'dispositif de formation qualifiante' (Favre, 2004: 39).

questions than answers. '*Instance réflexive, médiatrice par excellence, l'analyse des pratiques professionelles est un dispositif de questionnement plus que de résolution, régulé par du collectif dans une démarche polémique et coopérative*' (Favre, 2004: 63). By discussing the situations in the group – and by seeking solutions collectively – the *analyse de pratiques* contributes to the creation of a theoretical basis for pedagogic actions. With this position, Favre concurs with Hughes en MacNaughton (2000) and Dahlberg and Moss (2005: 4) when they – in following Deleuze and Guattarri – talk about 'minor politics', by which professionals, children and parents together create a new type of knowledge.

The training college in Lyon (ESSSE) has applied practical analysis within a module *Culture et Education* to deal with diversity in the services for young children (Malleval, 2004: 91-109; Mony, 2006: 49-64). The instructors at ESSSE make use of individual and group discussions in order to analyse the practical experiences and also use educational material that was produced within a European network working with the subject of diversity (DECET). The ESSSE institute has also applied the practical analysis to working in a mixed-gender team (Ndjapou, 2007).

According to Mony (2007: 15.32), professionalism demands a creative way of thinking: '*La capacité à trouver la situation unique dans chaque situation.*' In order to master this competency, all students receive, during their internship, the task to implement an original educational project that is based on a concrete practical question. Practical analysis is also used to interpret the preventive function that attempts to avoid stigmatization of the children and their parents (Mony 2007: 18.30).

5.5.4.2. Learning on the work floor

In the early 1990s, Verba studied the values and the cultural interests of the EJE, and came to the conclusion that the majority of the carers of young children came from the upper middle class. The EJEs appear to be typical for what Pierre Bourdieu calls the *petite bourgeoisie nouvelle*. This is the group that, according to Bourdieu, arose in the 1960s and adhered strongly to the values that are concerned with openness, liberation and communication (Verba, 2006: 96). Because of their adherence to these values, many EJEs took jobs in the *crèches parentales*. The parent-run crèches originated from the 'May '68' movement and were deeply connected to the value system of the EJE. The professionalism that was aspired to in the EJE training course also dovetailed with the socio-pedagogical project of the *crèches parentales*. (Verba, 2006: 186)[9]. In 1986, the federation of the parent-run crèches ACEPP (Association des Collectifs Enfants Parents Profesionnels) started – with the support of the Bernard van Leer Foundation and under the animated leadership of Josette Combes – a *programme interculturelle dans les quartiers d'habitat social*. (Cadart, 2005:31). ACEPP realized early on that, in order to be able to work in underprivileged neighborhoods, the *crèches parentales* needed – alongside of the EJE's – another type of staff member whose sphere of experience was closer to that of the parents who participated in these crèches. Myriam Mony, who was then responsible for the training department of ACEPP, therefore started an employment project of alternative learning for unemployed women living in these neighborhoods (Mony, 1993: 28). Within a European NOW project (European Social Fund), a collaborative effort was established with training colleges and social centres. These women returners and young unemployed persons follow a training trajectory of 3 to 4 years in the *crèches parentales*. First of all, they worked on the integration of the younger/unemployed in the crèche. Many of these women came from difficult personal circumstances and needed to find stability in their lives. They then commenced on a pre-qualification track. The candidates followed a course at ACEPP that was to prepare them for the entrance examination at the training colleges. At the same time, he/she was being trained on the work floor, under the supervision of an EJE, who had followed a special training course in coaching. If the candidate was then admitted, he/she could begin the training course either for *auxiliaire* or for EJE. The school for EJE took responsibility for the 950 hours of theory and the ACEPP for the 1400 hours of internship mentoring in the parent-run crèches (Mony, 1993: 29; 1994: 33). In her book on the history of the *crèches parentales*, Cadart writes that the influx of these people in the crèche was welcomed and provided the ne-cessary diversity among the personnel. 'La participation de personnes aux profils autres que ceux habituellement rencontrés dans les écoles conduisant aux métiers de la petite enfance est une vraie richesse pour les structures' (Cadart, 2006: 31). Via these *contrats de qualification*, the ACEPP was successful in pulling a large number of people out of unemployment, in helping them obtain qualifications and find work: between 1985 and 1995, 300 students were granted an EJE diploma and 80 received an *auxiliaire de puériculture* diploma (Cadart, 2006: 32). According to Verba (2006: 189), this *contrat de qualification*, was not welcomed by all professionals and training centres. Many teachers

---

9   Elsewhere (Peeters, 2003; 2005) we have shown that the *crèches parentales* – especially in the underprivileged neighborhoods – fulfill what Dahlberg, Moss and Pence call 'public forums': 'Early childhood institutions as public forums situated in civil society in which children and adults participate together in projects of social, cultural, political and economic significance' (Dahlberg, Moss and Pence, 1999: 73).

from the training institutes for EJE and *auxilliares* believed that the training course organized by ACEPP was inferior to the training courses that were organized solely by the schools.

In spite of these objections, the *contrats de qualifications* remained in existence and now other services also offer this course of education for the unemployed with no qualifications. Meanwhile, the ESSSE Institute in Lyon has been working for the past 19 years with the *contrat de qualification*. Many women of Arabic and African origin now use this track to obtain qualifications. Every other year, there are 40 candidates for 30 places. These participating candidates are supported by their employers. But it remains a difficult track that requires a firm commitment. The selection via this *contrat de qualification* is less fierce than among the students who, after completing their '*bac*', want to take on a study in the ESSSE. For 900 candidates for the EJE major, there are only 55 places. Every year, 600 young people want to commence with the study *auxiliaire de puériculture* for which only 60 places are available (Mony, 2007:26:30).

5.5.4.3. The new bachelor training course of 2005

The decree and the ruling of November 2005 concerning the *diplôme d'Etat d'éducateurs de jeunes enfants* extended the duration of the course to three years: 1500 hours of theoretical subjects and 2100 hours of practical work. With the extension of the course and the addition of new facets to the profile, a concession was made to the carers of young children who complained in the studies that their training was too short and must be substantively adjusted. In article 6 of the official text, it is pointed out that the practical internships are essential for acquiring the necessary competencies and that theory and practice must not be separated from each other (Ministère de l'Emploi, 2005:7). Thus, the significance of the *analyse de pratiques* is officially recognized.

The appendix to the ruling of November 2005 contains a professional profile in which the EJE is described as a social worker specialized in young children and whose tasks are set at three levels: child-rearing, prevention and coordination. The sectors in which the EJE is employable are extremely varied: hygiene and health, parental support, culture, relaxation and recreation, special needs children and all services providing care for young children.

One of the challenges for the EJE was, according to Meunier and Chétoui (2002 : 117) to find a better description of the how and why in the practice of their profession: '*Il est l'heure pour les EJE d'évaluer leurs pratiques, de mettre en exergue leurs compétences et de rendre enfin lisible à tous le pourqoui et le comment qui fondent l'utilité sociale d'une profession*' (Meunier en Chétoui, 2002: 140). For that reason, they advocate listing the required competencies and compiling a professional profile of the EJE.

The reform of 2005 conceded to this objection by introducing a competency based training (Mony, 2007:11.03) via the issuing of *un référentiel professionnel, et un référentiel de formation et de certification* (a professional profile, a training profile and a certification profile) in which the required tasks and competencies are integrated (Ministère de l'Emploi, 2005: 13).

With the reforms, connections – or *passerelles* – were also created that made horizontal mobility with other social professions possible (Ministère de l'Emploi, 2005: 31; Verba, 2006: 1; Mony, 2007: 17.30). Two of the four *domaines de formation* (*Communication professionnelle, Dynamiques institutionelles, inter-institutionelles et partenariales*) are the same for all social professions (*assistant de service sociale, conseiller en économie sociale familiale, éducateur technique spécialisé, animation*). The similarity with England, where they are striving to create a 'common core' (a collective group of educational domains) is striking. The EJE who wants to train for a different social profession, receives dispensation for this 'common core,' and is offered a lighter program for the other educational domains.

The decree and ruling concerning the new EJE training course of 2005 (art. 8) also makes verticle mobility possible. The *auxiliaires de puériculture* can complete the training course in one third of the normal time because they can receive dispensation for two thirds of the EJE course (Ministère de l' Emploi, 2005:8). In the ESSSE, the training institute in Lyon, the *auxiliaires en puériculture* who start the EJE course receive 300 hours dispensation (Mony, 2007: 24:30).

Because of the reforms, the EJE major also became a training course for managers (Verba, 2006: 155; Meunier & Chétoui; 2002: 135). The new training course gives child carers who work with young children the opportunity to move on to a management function. The training course *Educateur jeunes enfants* has, due to the reorganization, definitely become a course within the social professions: the *éducateur jeunes enfants* is now a social worker who counsels both the young child and the family (Verba, 2006: 1; Mony: 2007). The reorganization provided a new interpretation of professionalism: the educator of young children is given an extra task to support the social inclusion in a neighborhood (the social function of childcare). '*La professionnalité, c'est-à-dire la manière singulière d'exercer dans un contexte en fonction d'un projet et des situations rencontrées mobilise les capacités à porter attention à chacun et à construire une réponse d'accompagnement spéci-fique à chaque fois; elle mobilise aussi les capacités à fédérer une équipe et un ensemble de partenaires autour de l'enfant et de ses parents sur un territoire. Professionnels, au singulier et au pluriel les éducateurs de jeunes enfants sont chargés d'être acteurs privilégiés pour contribuer à tisser du lien social au service d'un projet éducatif d'inclusion sociale'* (Mony, 2006: 28).

5.5.5. The professionalism of the EJE: maverick or pioneer in Europe?

5.5.5.1. Is the EJE a reflective practitioner?

Within the research world, there is little contact between the French-language researchers and the colleagues who are more oriented toward the Anglo-Saxon literature (Bourgères, Vandenbroeck, 2007).[10] At the extremely popular conferences of the European Early Childhood Education Research Association, generally only a handful of French-speaking researchers are present. At the conference in Prague in 2007, there were 780 participants and only 6 delegates from France (EECERA, 2007). French-speaking researchers work with other concepts than their European colleagues: in this vein, for example, the notion of 'worker-researcher' or 'reflective practitioner' has not taken root in the French-lan-guage literature. For that reason, it seemed interesting to us to verify whether or not the EJE training course fits within the visions that are promoted by the more Anglo-Saxon-oriented authors such as Oberhuemer, Moss, Dahlberg and Rinaldi.

The professional profile uses – in the description of the functions – the verbs: *établir, élaborer, mettre en oeuvre, concevoir et conduire* (develop, explore, conceptualize, create, guide), which indicate that the EJE is not a technical executor of a curriculum or a qual-ity handbook, but someone who interprets his/her task in an autonomous and creative manner.

---

10 Typical for the gap between the French-speaking and Anglo-Saxon research worlds is the fact that the impor-tance of the EJE training course is hardly alluded to in international English-language overviews (Oberhuemer, Ullich, 1997; OECD, 2006), while, on the other hand, a French researcher specialized in staff training for early childhood education states with great conviction that, in the other European countries, there are no training courses for childcare staff members that are at the same level as the EJE in France. (Verba, 2006: 248).

Characteristic for the EJE training course is the *analyse de pratiques*. The visions of the French authors (Fablet, Favre, Meunier, Mallevalle, Doucet-Dahlgren, 2004) who documented this method of *analyse de pratiques* associate themselves with the practice applied in the pedagogics of Reggio Emilia. 'Professional development can be organized in such a way that it brings together men and women from all walks of life who are looking for new meaning and new values both within and beyond the conventional boundaries.' (Rinaldi, 2005:136).

The EJE, who is constantly analyzing concrete situations in dealing with children, parents and other professionals in order to come to effective solutions, is closely affiliated to the 'worker-researcher' or the 'reflective practitioner' as described by Moss (2003), or democratic professionalism as described by Oberhuemer (2005). By asking the student or educator to analyse elements from their professional practice, they are forced to first objectify their experiences and then to place their insights within a new theoretical framework (Doucet-Dahlgren, 2004: 78). Moss states that the 'reflective practitioner' or the 'worker as researcher' is a person who co-constructs knowledge. 'Co-construction involves creating knowledge in relationship with others, but also with theories, concepts and analyses from many different fields; in short, through frequent border crossing' (Moss, 2006: 36). On the basis of the professional profile, of the literature on the *analyse de pratiques* (Fablet, 2004 ed.), of one's own experiences during guest lectures and workshops in ESSSE in Lyon – one of the training institutes for *éducateur jeunes enfants* – and on the basis of the interview with Myrian Mony, director of the ESSSE training institute[11], we come to the conclusion that the training for carers of young children actually does form the students into 'reflective practitioners' or 'workers as researchers.'

5.5.5.2. Challenges for the future

Starting in the late 1950s, France commenced with an evolution in which a completely different interpretation of professionalism was given to the profession of *éducateur jeunes enfants* and to the *professeur écoles maternelles*. This evolution drove the *écoles maternelles* and the childcare sector further apart and provided a 'split system' (OECD, 2006) between school and childcare in which each of the structures have nothing to do

---

11 Mony (2007: 16.00), director of the EJE training course in Lyon, states that the EJE training course in all of the training institutes in France is one that produces 'reflective practitioners'.

with the other. The huge differentiation in the methods of dealing with young children was, however, unjustifiable for many researchers, parents and professionals (Verba, 2005: 101; Mony, 2007). During the past few years, there has been a great deal of criticism of the one-sided didactic approach to young children in the écoles maternelles (Bachelet, Mozére, 2004: 213).

The *éducateur jeunes enfants* should, according to their social pedagogical background, be able to make an important contribution in involving the parents of the young children in the operation of the *écoles maternelles*, especially in the case of very young children. Verba (2005: 254) as well as Mony (2007: 6.40) feel that it is a priority that an investment is made in the transition between crèche and school. The EJEs play an extremely positive role in a number of these *passerelle* projects, including the one in Lyon (Mony, 2007: 8.00). Moreover, a certain amount of willingness can be found among the *Féderation des écoles maternelles* to collaborate with other actors who work with young children – including the EJEs – in the underprivileged neighborhoods (Mony, 2007: 8.15).

Alongside of this, an effort must be made to attract more men to the EJE training course. The projects that are being undertaken by, among others, the ESSSE Institute in Lyon to make the training course more male-friendly are a promising beginning (Ndjabou, 2007)[12].

5.5.6. Conclusion

In the early 1970s, two diplomas were required in France in the childcare sector that gave professionalism in the occupations concerning young children a strong emphasis on the medical-hygienic aspects. Due to the establishment of the new training course *éducateur jeunes enfants* in higher education, there was a reshaping in France towards an educational professionalism that later evolved into a socio-pedagogical interpretation of professionalism: the support of families and the shaping of the idea of inclusion in underprivileged neighborhoods. This social function is high on the agenda of international organizations such as the OECD (OECD, 2006: 213-215) and requires a different interpretation of professionalism. In this context, the training course *éducateur jeunes enfants* is inspiring and unique because such countries as Denmark, Sweden, New Zealand and Italy, which all have high-quality training courses at the bachelor's and master's

---

12 See the ESSSE project supported by the Bernard van Leer Foundation: 'Genre et Mixité dans l' éducation des jeunes enfants.'

levels, are more focused on the educational aspect and place less emphasis on the social function of childcare and kindergarten.

A second interesting point is concerned with the horizontal and vertical mobility within the French qualification structure. In France, they have succeeded in developing a qualification structure that is simple and transparent.[13] Non-qualified target group staff members can enter the childcare sector and have the possibility to follow a *contrat de qualification* that can lead to a diploma of *auxiliaire de puériculture* or to a bachelor's degree (EJE).

The revised EJE training course is also an inspiring example because the mentoring of non-qualified staff members via the method of the *analyse de pratique* has been included in the competency profile (Ministère de l' Emploi, 2005: 29).

In France, mentors who work with young children can be given dispensation if they want to obtain the EJE diploma and, after having acquired this diploma, can move up to a management function.

In the third chapter we found that there is a consensus within the research world that childcare needs 'reflective practitioners'. The French system can be an inspiration in this area because, alongside of the *auxiliaires de puériculture* – with a more technical interpretation of professionalism – it also places the social pedagogue *éducateur jeunes enfants*.

This course – as has been proven from the literature study, from interviews and from concrete experiences with students – shapes the EJE into 'reflective practitioners' or 'worker-researchers' (Moss, 2003) and is based on a 'democratic professionalism' (Oberhuemer, 2005).

---

13   This is in comparison to the English qualification framework that is extremely complex and hardly transparent
     at all.

5.6. New-Zealand: The construction of a new profession

5.6.1. Methodology

Our first contact with childcare in New Zealand dates from 1991 when we attended a conference of the International Family Day Care Organisation in Sydney. At the conference,
it was clear that the development of an 'Ethical Code' for the professions involving young
children was an important theme in Australia and New Zealand (Peeters, 1991:16). It was
not until 2004 that regular contact was developed with colleagues from New Zealand.
At the conference of the European Early Childhood Education Research Association in
Malta, there was a delegation from New Zealand and the important developments in the
New Zealand pre-school sector were illuminated in a key-note address (Carr, Rameka,
2005). During this conference, we took part in a Special Interest Group (SIG) on 'professionalism' that was initiated by Carmen Dalli, associate professor at Victoria University
of Wellington (NZ). This SIG network and, in particular, the contact with Professor Dalli,
gave us the opportunity to delve more deeply into the most significant developments in
connection with professionalism in New Zealand.

In November 2004, we were invited – together with the New Zealander Ross Boyd (2004) –
to give a lecture at the conference ' Learning with other Countries' for the National Day
Care Trust in the Westminster Conference Centre in London. At the time Ross Boyd was
Education Policy Manager at the Ministry of Education and had responsibility for the
implementation of the 'New Zealand Strategic Plan for Early Childhood Education'. In
the conference corridors, we had fascinating discussions on a segment of this Strategic
Plan that stipulated that all staff working with young children between the ages of 0 and
5 were, by 2012, to have a bachelor's degree or three-year graduate qualification. Moreover, within the editorial offices of the journal *Children in Europe*, the editor-in-chief,
Prof. Moss – who visited New Zealand on a regular basis – introduced the subject of the
country's inspiring interpretation of professionalism. In early 2007, we were invited, via
Dr. Sarah Farquhar (editor and publisher of the journal *NZ Research in ECE*) and the
Early Childhood Council (ECC), one of the largest umbrella organisations for childcare
centres in New-Zealand, to give a keynote address during the annual ECC conference
and this provided me with an ideal opportunity to study the New Zealand model at close
hand and to include it in this study.

During the conference, the Minister of Education, Steve Maharey (Labour Party), explained his government's policy and we heard the critical comments by Katherine Rich of

the National Party (opposition) and the reactions of the director of the Early Childhood Council, Sue Thorn, to the reforms. At Victoria University in Wellington, we interviewed Sue Cherrington, the Head of the School for Early Childhood Teacher Education and Prof. Carmen Dalli. We also visited a Kohanga Reo, a Maori centre for young children and their parents in Napier, where we had a discussion with two male staff members in training.

5.6.2. History: the paradigm of diversity as the guiding principle

The history of Aotearoa-New Zealand is characterized by the diversity of its population. The Maoris came to the islands 1000 years ago and the Europeans (the Pahekas, as the Maoris called them) settled on the two islands in the 19th century. After World War II, many inhabitants from Asia, Africa and the Pacific Islands also immigrated to New Zealand. This paradigm of diversity also had a huge impact on the history of the provisions for young children (May, 2002: 1).

5.6.2.1. Working towards a diversity of provisions

Just as in many European countries, (Humblet, 1998; Vandenbroeck, 2004) the provisions for young children in New Zealand came into being at the end of the 19th century as care facilities for young children from poor families. The State had little interest in these provisions, but after World War II this attitude started to change. While in 1944, only 3.4% of all children went to the 'Kindergartens' (at that time, the only facility that was supported by the government), by 1999, no fewer than 59% of all children attended one of the many types of facilities for young children. (May, 2002: 3).

This expansion of participation was accompanied by a diversification of early childhood provisions. The primary facility for 3 and 4 year olds was still the Kindergarten service which was fully funded by the government and staffed by qualified teachers. Kindergartens, however, were open for half days and, as more women entered the paid workforce in the seventies and eighties, it became increasingly difficult for the kindergartens to satisfy the new needs of parents. Therefore, childcare facilities were established that provided care from morning till evening and for which the staff was underqualified and underpaid. (Boyd, 2005: 22). The underfunded and underpaid nature of this workforce was accompanied by low social appreciation for those who worked with young children (Dalli, 1993: 224).

Another part of the early childhood sector includes playcentres, which were established in the mid-forties and uphold a philosophy in which parents are deeply involved in their children's learning, and more recently, indigenous early childhood services, Te Kohanga Reo and Pacific Islands language groups. This final group of services was established in the 1980s from a concern that the language and culture of the indigenous Maori and that of their Pacific neighbours were being eroded within an education system based on European-based knowledge and culture. Te Kohanga Reo centres, and the Pacific Islands Centres or the so-called 'language nests' have a broader mission than traditional centres for young children: they endeavour to give children and their parents language immersion in the Maori language, or in one of the languages in the South Pacific Islands. 'These programmes were positioned outside of the existing education agencies and organizations, which were deemed to have failed Maori children' (May, 2002:6).

The diversity of the childcare facilities was further expanded by the development of a number of specific services for children: the 'home-based centres' (services for family day carers), the centres for occasional care, the provisions with a specific pedagogical approach (Steiner, Montessori) and even a 'distant learning centre for young children' as part of the Correspondence School service (May, 2002:3).

5.6.2.2. Integration within education

According to Professor Helen May (2002:3), one of the leading scholars of the Early Childhood Education sector in New Zealand and past Director (1996-2000) of the Institute for Early Childhood Studies at Victoria University of Wellington, the modern Early Childhood Education policy was strongly influenced by efficient and intensive lobbying by the sector and by academics. This influence put Early Childhood Education on the political agenda on a regular basis. Both the Labour Governments (centre left) and the National Party governments reacted in the same way to this efficient lobbying, namely by giving a number of academics the commission to work with the sector in formulating a body of recommendations for new policy within the Early Childhood Education sector. The first advisory report for the government was the so-called 'Bailey Report' from 1947 (Report of the Consultative Committee on Preschool Education Services). This report advocated that the State should take on all the provisions for young children in order to deal summarily with the 'mothering' atmosphere that was characteristic for the sector during that period. The government did not accept the recommendations of this report and, as yet, the Early Childhood Education sector is a mixed sector in which the initiative is based on private facilities and local community groups.

In 1986, all of the various types of provisions were brought under the authority of the Department of Education, a policy agency that, in itself, does not offer any services for young children. New Zealand therefore became one of the first countries to replace the 'split system model in the early years policy' (Bennet, 2003), in which childcare falls under the authority of Welfare and the pre-schools under the authority of Education, with a system in which the services for 'care' and services for 'education' were integrated. In this way, New Zealand deals summarily with the alleged discrepancies between care and education that still exist in many European countries (including Belgium and France). This integration of the various services under Education enabled a number of positive consequences further down the track including a rationalisation of government funding across all services and the creation of quality criteria (child ratios and qualifications of staff) that were applied across the full range of services. Shortly after the integration of the administration of care and education services within one government agency, in 1988, integrated three-year training courses were introduced in colleges of education for those wanting to work with children between the ages of 0 and 5: 'This meant that early childhood teacher education courses at the colleges of education now started to produce graduates who could work in any part of early childhood education services' (Dalli, 1999:56).

In 1988, the report commissioned by the then Labour government under the chairmanship of Dr. Anne Meade, 'Education to be More', was published. About this, Meade herself said: 'The political gains made by early childhood in 1989 were made possible through the co-ordinated activities of women, unions, Maori and people from other ethnic communities' (in Dalli, 1993: 225). This so-called 'Meade Report' was an important philosophical statement on Equity, and it was based on a belief in the advantages of Early Childhood Education for children, parents and their communities, as well as for the broader society. The report was also important because it emphasized 'the holistic nature of early childhood care and education' (May, 2002: 6). In 'Before Five' – the answer from the labour government to the Meade Report – most of the demands were accepted, also the demand to provide better qualified personnel and subsidies for the training of non-qualified personnel. According to Dalli, 'Before Five' had an important impact on the personnel policy in the provisions; many of the centres made use of the more favourable subsidy regulations in order to upgrade the qualifications of their personnel. (Dalli, 1999: 3).

At the end of 1990, the conservatives (National Party) came to power once again and a period of cut-backs ensued. Dalli expressed it as follows: 'Early Childhood Education returned to being the Cinderella of the Education sector' (Dalli, 1993). Because the government invested less in the sector, the commercial childcare centres were able to expand greatly. The new government also scaled back the training requirements, which caused great confusion and an enormous amount of dissatisfaction within the educational world.

The optimism of the late 1980s within the sector had declined sharply but, nonetheless, there were two developments that were able to inspire the sector: the curriculum *Te Whaariki* and the Code of Ethics.

5.6.2.3. 'Weaving an early childhood curriculum'

In 1991, the National Party government appointed a team, under the leadership of two respected university researchers, Margaret Carr and Helen May, whose task it was to develop a common curriculum for all provisions for children between the ages of 0 and 5. Working as a team with two representatives of the Maori Te Kohanga Reo Trust, Tilly Reedy and Dr. Tamati Reedy, these two researchers developed a curriculum that was strongly influenced by Maori culture (Carr, Rameka, 2005, 6). Within the team, a lively and intense cooperation was, namely, instigated with them. The developers of the curriculum wanted to put together a bi-cultural document in which Maori visions of children and western concepts were integrated. 'This Maori perspective links children to the land and to the past' (Carr, Rameka, 2005). The central aspect of the Maori vision is the *mana* of the child, a concept that encompasses self-respect, prestige, power, strength and appreciation all in one word. According to Tilly Reed, 'having *mana* at their disposal' is a means for children to determine their own fate (Carr, Rameka, 2005: 6). Five domains of *mana* were developed in the Maori language and in English, without this being considered a true translation (May, 2002: 11).

Mana atua	Well-being
Mana whenua	Belonging
Mana tagata	Contribution
Mana reo	Communication
Mana ao turoa	Exploration

Guided by these principles, the *Te Whaariki* curriculum articulates clear aspirations for children: 'to grow up as competent and confident learners and communicators'. *Te Whaariki*, at the same time, provides a framework for the training of 'early years workers' (Carr, Rameka, 2005: 6). *Te Whaariki* differs fundamentally from traditional Western curricula that are based on the motorial, intellectual, emotional and social development of the child. 'It integrates education, social and cultural outcomes, and positions the child as an active learner in the early childhood centre, in their family and as part of the wider community' (Boyd, 2005: 22).

Te Whaariki is, however, also a political statement on racism and children: the individuality of children, their ethnicity and their rights within the New-Zealand society are central to this curriculum. '*Te Whaariki* provided a curriculum space where languages and culture could be in the foreground and not an add-on' (Mara in May, 2002: 12).

The name *Te Whaariki* refers to a mat that gives support for standing ('a mat for all to stand on') into which each early childhood service can 'weave' a curriculum based on its individual character.

The principles and objectives that are defined in this document form a framework that offers the opportunity for various types of facilities to 'weave' according to their own pattern. 'It describes a 'spider web' model of curriculum for children, in contrast to a 'step' model. The 'step or staircase' model conjures up the images of a series of independent steps that lead to a platform where the child exists and at which point measurable outcomes can be identified. The *Te Whaariki* model views the curriculum for each child more like a 'spider web' or weaving and emphasises a model of knowledge and understanding for young children as being a tapestry of increasing complexity and richness' (May, Carr, 1996: 3).

The *Te Whaariki* metaphor assumes that there is a strongly motivated 'reflective practitioners' attitude within the early childhood settings. The curriculum does not contain any concrete guidelines that can be easily implemented, but the services themselves are expected to provide the content of this curriculum. In 1997 the Government's Education Review Office (ERO) carried out a study on the manner in which the curriculum was implemented and ascertained that the sector was enthusiastic about *Te Whaariki*, but that they were lacking in confidence to implement it. 'There would need to be on-going professional development in a sector that had large numbers of untrained or poorly trained staff.' (May, 2002: 12). The sector was also lacking the necessary resources to raise the qualifications of many staff employed in the sector. Moreover, the holistic and bi-cultural basis of *Te Whaariki* was a major challenge which posed problems for a large number of the centres. The staff was used to working with the traditional vision of play activities and the *Te Whaariki* approach made them unsure of themselves. In 2003, Cullen evaluated how the teachers were dealing with the *Te Whaariki* curriculum and came to the same conclusions. She determined that there were three domains in which the teachers were having problems: dealing with diversity; the holistic vision of the child and a clear comprehension the 'professional knowledge base of the teacher' (Scrivens, 2005).

The introduction of the *Te Whaariki* once again placed the professionalism of the staff on the agenda.

5.6.2.4. The 'Code of Ethics'

The project 'The Early Childhood Code of Ethics for Aotearoa/New Zealand' was instigated in 1993 by Carmen Dalli and Linda Mitchell. A few years earlier, a 'code of ethics' had already been developed in Australia under the chairmanship of Anne Stonehouse (Peeters, 1991). Dalli and Mitchell were also inspired by the work in this area that was being done in the United States and in British Columbia (Dalli, Cherringhton, 1994: 1). They started a national work group that received support from FECEO, an umbrella of Early Childhood organizations, and from OMEP Aotearoa-New-Zealand (Organisation Mondiale de l'Education Prescolaire). According to Dalli (1999: 64) the activities concerning the Code of Ethics developed into an action research investigation that involved the practicing professionals in every step of the planning phase and in the activities that were undertaken. Two years later, the Code was launched at the 6th Early Childhood Convention (Dalli and Mitchell, 1995).

An ethical code is often seen as the clearest indication of professionalism, and a way in which to promote the status of a profession. By using a 'code of ethics', the professional in question knows the difference between the correct way of acting and the way that is only pragmatic (Katz, 1978, in Dalli and Mitchell, 1995: 8).

For the sector, the development of a 'code of ethics' was the proof that, within the Early Childhood Education community, there was an explicit commitment to steer and improve the pedagogical practices and to make a public statement on the values that are the basis for pedagogical practice. (Dalli, 1999: 7).

In 1994, Dalli and Cherrington sent a questionnaire to 600 early childhood centres requesting a response from a qualified staff member. The idea was to collect information on the frequency and type of ethical dilemmas confronting the staff members. Based on 322 respondents who filled in the extensive questionnaire, the researchers concluded that the professionals felt that ethical dilemmas were extremely important and that they felt that the development of a Code of Ethics was certainly worthwhile. The great diversity of dilemmas that the respondents identified provides evidence of the complexity of working with young children. Most of the ethical dilemmas occurred in the relationships among the parents and in the relationships between the parents and the staff members (Dalli and Cherrington, 1994: 14).

FECEO and OMEP New Zealand were given the task of developing the Code even further. In New Zealand, there is no professional organization to which all teachers belong; because of that, the Code had to be formally accepted by all the childcare organisations (Dalli, 1999: 65). In 2003, Dalli ascertained that there was still no professional body that was entrusted with the monitoring of the Code. For that reason, it was unclear whether or not the Code was being used effectively: 'We do not know whether or not the Code is in vigorous use' (Dalli, 2003: 11).

But the New Zealand Teacher's Council, the professional and regulatory body for teachers, supports maintenance of professional standards through competencies and discipline processes. While these standards are not a Code of Ethics, they could be seen to serve a similar purpose (Lequesne, 2007).

5.6.2.5. 'Pathways to the Future: Ngä Huarahi Arataki'

In September 2002, the New Zealand government launched the policy document *Pathways to the Future: a ten year strategic plan for early childhood education 2002-2012* (Ministry of Education, 2002). In this document, the government made three policy objectives a priority: increasing participation in quality early childhood education, improving the quality of ECE services and promoting collaborative relationships. With this policy plan, the New Zealand government associated itself with the Scandinavian Welfare Model (Esping Andersen, 2000). 'The principled statements about universal entitlement to early childhood services suggest that the current Government sees its role as fitting within the tradition of a social democratic welfare state model of government where entitlements draw on the universal rights of social citizenship' (Dalli and Te One, 2003: 183).

Pathways to the Future was the result of a workgroup, chaired by Dr. Anne Meade, set up by the Minister of Education and made up of 31 representatives from the sector who consulted widely with their constituent groups. Thirteen hundred recommendations were incorporated into the final report. The then Minister of Education, Trevor Mallard, wanted to use this 10 Year Strategic Plan to enable all the facilities for children between the ages of 0 and 5 to implement the *Te Whaariki* curriculum. At the same time, the Minister wanted to increase the professionalism of the staff members over a period of 10 years: 'Early childhood teachers who meet and maintain the same professional standards as school teachers' (Mallard, 2002: 1). According to Ross Boyd, Ministry of Education policy manager, this approach ensured that the 10 Year Strategy was supported by the sector and became, therefore, 'a powerful vehicle for change' (Boyd, 2004:23). Dalli and Te One noted that 'The goal in *Pathways to the Future* of improving the quality of ECE services, was widely welcomed by the sector.' It was, in particular, the measures to upgrade the qualifications of the teachers and to make teacher registration obligatory that were met with great approval in the sector. (Dalli & Te One, 2003:189).

The first measure to upgrade the qualifications consisted of requiring a three-year Teaching Diploma (three-year training course) or Bachelor degree-level qualification for all new 'persons responsible' (mainly management staff but often also hands-on teachers), starting from 2002. In order to support this requirement, 'incentive grants' were provided by the government so that all staff seeking to upgrade their qualifications could apply to the New Zealand Qualification Authority to have their qualifications and teaching experience assessed before embarking on an upgrade programme through one of five teacher-training institutions which developed special teacher-education programs that took into account earlier acquired competencies and qualifications (Recognition of Prior Learning). Within these initiatives to upgrade the qualifications, a special effort was made to recruit Maori and Pacifika students by making special scholarships available to them. (Dalli, 2003: 191-192).

In June 2004, the New Zealand government published new measures in which important financial support was given to the facilities in order to enable the non-qualified personnel to take the Bachelor's training course. By 2012[14], 70% of all staff members must have a teacher's diploma at the Bachelor's level and the remaining 30% must be enrolled in a teacher's college. Moreover, the salaries of the 'early childhood teachers' are being brought up to the same level as the salaries of elementary school teachers. This has proven to be the most important motivation for the staff to take the teacher training course. (Boyd, 2005: 23).

Dalli and Te One point out that the private commercial sector and the 'community-based' sector have different visions concerning the implementation of *Pathways to the Future*. The representatives of the private sector (primarily the Early Childhood Council) feel that

---

14 In late 2007, this deadline was extended to 2013.

the governmental measures to upgrade the quality and the upgrading of the qualification requirements are an attempt by the government to take over the private sector (Dalli and Te One, 2003: 187). Linda Mitchell studied the differences between the private and the 'community-based' sectors and came to the conclusion that, as a whole, the private sector scored lower for important quality criteria: 'Training and qualification of staff, high rates of staff pay, high staff/child ratios and small group size' (Mitchell, 2002:2). Mitchell, therefore, pointed out the importance of the measures to upgrade the qualifications of the staff members in the private sector (Mitchell, 2002:13). Many in the private and commercial part of the ECE sector do support the qualification requirements, but the Early Childhood Council has questioned the recommendations for upgrading the qualifications of the staff members. Speaking at the annual conference of The Early Childhood Council, the majority of whose members are private providers of early childhood services, La Rocque formulated his criticism as follows: The recommendations in *Pathways to the Future* that 100% of teachers be registered by 2012 may have unintended consequences, ... small private providers may be forced out of the market ... and families may be forced into the unregulated part of ECE' (La Rocque in Dalli, Te One, 2003: 188).

This discrepancy between the private commercial and the 'community-based' sectors continues to exist today. At the most recent conference of the Early Childhood Council in March 2007, we experienced firsthand how intense the discussions were on a new measure by the Labour government. The government wants to provide 20 hours per week of free Early Childhood Education for all three and four-year olds. They anticipate an increase in the subsidies for this, but the commercial sector – as expressed by the Early Childhood Council (Sue Thorn) and supported in this by Katerine Rich of the conservative 'National Party' – claim that this compensation is too small to completely cover the costs of the facilities in the more expensive neighbourhoods. They, therefore, object to the fact that the commercial centres are not allowed to charge the parents extra for the 'free 20 hours'. The 'community-based' sector supports the measures of the Education Ministry, aimed at increasing the accessibility of the facilities for less-privileged children and their parents.

5.6.3. Home-based care: even New Zealand has its paradox

The sector of the private childcare workers, or Home-based Early Childhood Education is, in New Zealand, a recognised branch of the Early Childhood Education sector, and is subject to the same curriculum *Te Whaariki*. Nonetheless, the educational requirements of the Strategic Plan apply solely to the coordinators of the services (the service managers) and not to the family daycare caregivers themselves.

5.6.3.1. How did this paradox come about?

The Family Day Care Networks originated in New Zealand as local neighbourhood initiatives (community groups) in the 1970s. Just as in Belgium (Vandenbroeck, 2004), during a period of economic recession, financial arguments played a part in the decision of the government to recognize this form of childcare: 'Family Day Care neatly filled a gap in the childcare market by providing supervised full-day childcare places for young children at little additional cost to the government' (Everiss, 1999: 4). Just as in Belgium and other European countries, there were fierce debates in the 1970s and 1980s on whether or not Family Day Care was a form of childcare equivalent to centre-based provisions.

During the 1980s, most of the New Zealand Family Day Care Schemes (networks of family daycare services which provide infrastructural support for individual family daycare caregivers working in their own home who had associated themselves with a large charity welfare organisation (Barnardos), that, via 'home-based care' provided parenting support to vulnerable families). Because of the transfer of all services for young children to the educational sector in 1986, the Family Day Care Schemes could obtain subsidies directly from the Ministry of Education. Barnardos resisted this transfer to 'education,' but the services were no longer dependent upon Barnardos; many 'schemes' left the charitable organization and made the transfer to Education (Everiss, 1999: 11).

The Meade Report advised the government to provide more services with access to subsidies and, at the same time, to link the subsidies to quality standards. 'The impact of these two policies on family day care was remarkable. From an underfunded poor relation within a poorly funded sector, family day care, with its high enrolment of under-two-years-olds, suddenly found itself at the wealthier end of the spectrum of ECE services' (Everiss and Dalli, 2003: 64).

The 1990s were a period of challenge and change for 'home-based' Early Childhood Education. Family Day Care became the fastest-growing branch of Early Childhood Education in New Zealand. Between 1990 en 2000, the number of children in 'home-based services' rose from 1611 to 8937; an increase of 450%. Nonetheless, the percentage of children in 'home-based' Early Childhood Education in New Zealand remains limited:

family daycare caregivers care for only 5% of the children of pre-school age (Everiss and Dalli, 2003:59). The sector took important steps to develop quality standards and also took initiatives to set up special training courses for family daycare caregivers. The Home-based Care Order was developed, which set down standards which included child safety and child/adult ratios. Family Day Care was incorporated into the Statement of Desirable Objectives and Practices, by which family daycare caregivers who are affiliated with a 'scheme' (Service for private childcare workers) are regularly assessed for quality. At the same time, starting in 1996, the services were subject to the requirements of the *Te Whaariki* curriculum.

'The new regulatory policies of the 90s indicate that, at least at the level of policy, family day care was being conceptualised as a sector that could be regulated to achieve standards of professional activity similar to the centre-based care part of the sector' (Dalli, 2003:6). Moss also recognizes the importance of the integration of childcare by family daycare caregivers into the New Zealand Education system: 'Two conditions may be particularly important in fostering professionalization: the bringing of childcare, including family daycare, fully into the education system; and the incorporation of family daycare within a comprehensive system of public funding' (Moss, 2003: 237).

5.6.3.2. Training initiatives have a limited impact

The sector was in complete evolution in the area of training courses, as well: in 1994, the specialized training course 'New Zealand certificate in Family Day Care: caregiver' was recognized by the New Zealand Qualifications Authority.

This certificate covers a two-year study that consists of 6 modules of 50 hours of course work each, 50 hours of practical assignments and one introductory module of 20 hours of course work and 20 hours of practical assignments.

In New Zealand, it is clear that, among the researchers (Everiss, 1999; Dalli, 2003) as well as in the sector itself (NZ Family Day Care Association: 2003; NZ Home-based ECE Association: 2003), there is a consensus concerning the fact that training is important in order to secure the newly attained status of Family Day Care within the Early Childhood Education sector.

In 1998, Everiss surveyed family daycarers about their views on training courses. The majority of respondents perceived a specialized training course as a necessity and said that they were prepared to take such a course if they had the necessary support for it (Everiss,

1999: 23). Everiss quoted numerous authors who stated that it was not experience, but rather training and education that correlated most closely with quality care for young children: 'Other studies from home-based caregivers which have used education, experience, and training as variables to measure caregiver competence, have indicated that the effects of training are strong and positive' (Eheart, Leavitt, 1986 cited in Everiss, 1999: 22). Everiss added: 'While training was associated with more sensitive care, care-giving experience was not; providers with more experience were rated as more detached and harsher' (Galinsky et al., 1994).

Figures from the Ministry of Education provide, however, a completely different picture: seventy-five percent of the family daycarers has taken at least one of the modules of the New Zealand certificate of Family Day Care. In practice, this is generally the required introductory module (20 hours of course work and 20 hours of practical assignments). Only 11% had taken all of the modules, and 17% had no qualifications whatsoever (Everiss and Dalli, 2003:71). The researchers, therefore, decided that the policy-makers would have to take measures to stimulate family daycarers to take more training courses and to implement those training systems that recognized previously attained competencies.

5.6.4. Conclusion

Up until the end of the 1980s, New Zealand had to deal with the problem of the low level of professionalism among those employed in the care and education of the youngest children (0 to 3 years old) (Boyd, 2004: 22). The manner in which this country, with its 4 million inhabitants, tackled this paradox can serve as an inspiration for other countries that are in a process of professionalization. During the past twenty years, and through close collaboration with the academic world, the Early Childhood sector in New Zealand has been successful in placing the upgrading of professionalism of staff members in the services for pre-school education on the political agenda.

The way New Zealand has implemented its reforms is exemplary for the manner in which a country – via a democratic approach – can achieve the development of new knowledge. 'Democracy creates the possibility for diversity to flourish. By so doing, it offers the best environment for the production of new thinking and new practice, and so for society to enable and value cultural and paradigmatic pluralism' (Moss, 2007: 3).

In New Zealand, since World War II, the various actors within the Early Childhood Education sector have been in continuous dialogue with 'policy makers' and dedicated researchers whose objective it is to collect new knowledge on the interpretation of professionalism: the development of a collective training course for those working in childcare and kindergarten in 1988; the development of the multicultural curriculum *Te Whaariki* and the collaborative development of a Code of Ethics in the 1990s. This successful collaboration reached its pinnacle in 2002 when the government commissioned representatives of the sector – under the chairmanship of eminent researcher Dr. Anne Meade – to develop *Pathways to the Future, a ten year strategic plan.* One of the objectives of this strategic plan is to have all staff members in the sector (also those working with the 2 to 3-year-olds group) trained at the bachelor's level by the year 2012.

In New Zealand, the political world has a great interest in the level of the education of the staff members working in Early Childhood Education. There, politicians are convinced that only those people who are highly educated are able to offer quality services to parents and children (Boyd, 2005). In several European countries, politicians are more inclined to advocate an upgrade in the capacity of the childcare by employing even more untrained personnel. It will be a great challenge to convince the politicians that the creation of 'quality jobs' and the offering of high-quality services to children and their parents must be on the political agenda.

The uniqueness of the New Zealand model is that they have succeeded in creating – from the perspective of diversity (*Te Whaariki*) – a new body of knowledge on the manner in which professionalism is to be interpreted. In Denmark, a country with a high level of professionalism, dealing with diversity, for example, remains one of the weak points in the system (Christensen, 2007). New Zealand has taken on the challenge to combine diversity with a 'reflective practitioners' model. *Te Whaariki* formulates general principles on the manner in which one can deal with diversity between the children and the parents and the practitioner is asked to design his own approach for dealing with this problem in practice. Also, the way in which *Te Whaariki* came about within a 'communicative space' is inspiring. The on-going democratic cooperation between Maori, Pacifica and Paheka specialists and people from the sector has led to unique results.

New Zealand is fascinating with respect to the cooperation between the private-commercial sector and the 'community-based' sector. The government has taken measures to provide equal treatment to private and 'community-based' ECE: a private centre can apply for practically the same subsidy from the national government as a community centre. There are also identical training requirements for both sectors. The KIWI model has already proven that it is possible to set high qualification requirements for the private sector. At the same time, however, the New Zealand experience has taught us that the chasm between the commercial and the 'community-based' sectors is difficult to bridge. In spite of subsidization on a par with community-based early childhood services, the commercial sector in New Zealand continues to have difficulties implementing the social function of ECE.

5.7. Denmark: the 'pedagogue' model: care in the broadest sense of the word; daily life as a pedagogical environment for children

5.7.1. Method followed

In June 1991, three colleagues and I visited the facilities for children in Aarhus in Denmark. The visit was organized by Claus Jensen, a staff member at BUPL, the organization for 'pedagogues' in Denmark. We were there for a full week and we visited various types of organizations, day-care centres, age-integrated centres (0 to 12 years old), kindergartens and also the Jydsk Paedagog-Seminarium in Aarhus. This visit made a great impression on all of us. The training course for 'pedagogue' that was 3.5 years long, was, on the one hand, strongly theoretical and based on a pedagogical vision and, on the other hand, it was an extremely creative course which included a great emphasis on music-making, theater and expressive art forms (Somers, 1991:6-7). In the evenings, after the visits, there were intense discussions with Claus Jensen and also with Jytte Jensen, researcher at the Paedagog-Seminarium, on the particularly fascinating interpretation of professionalism of the Danish 'pedagogue.'

In 1992, a conference was held in Copenhagen, under the auspices of the European Commission, called *Parental Employment and Caring for Children: Policies and Services in EC and Nordic Countries* in which the Danish model was discussed in great detail. (Social Ministeriet, 1993). Within the framework of this conference, a visit was made to the school for pedagogues in Copenhagen. This visit gave us the opportunity to broaden our insights concerning the training course for 'pedagogues.'

After these visits, there was regular contact with Claus Jensen and Jytte Jensen and a collaborative project was also developed: VBJK was to take on the Dutch production of 'Can you feel colours?' a video on the Danish vision of childcare. In the years to come, there would be continued regular contact with the Danish colleagues at conferences and European gatherings.

Starting in 2001, we worked on a structured basis with BUPL (the organization of pedagogues) in the editorial board of *Children in Europe*. VBJK is responsible for the Dutch edition *Kinderen in Europa* and BUPL publishes the Danish version: *Børn i Europe*. The network of journals that publishes *Children in Europe* comes together once or twice a year for an editorial meeting. But, alongside of that, the partners in the network also see each other at conferences that are organized by the members of the network and at which other partners are invited as guest speakers. The Danish model of professionalism is, because of both its originality and its excellent quality, often a subject at these conferences and also in the articles in *Children in Europe* (Honge, 2003; Lund, 2005; Damgaard, 2006; Jensen, Hansen, 2003).

In 2003 and 2007, the editorial meetings were held in Copenhagen on the premises of the organization of 'pedagogues'. This gives us the opportunity to come into contact with the many activities that this organisation undertakes in order to increase the level of professionalism among its members.

All of these opportunities provide us with numerous possibilities to continue to follow, firsthand, the evolution in the training for the profession of 'pedagogue'. The discussion that we had in 2004 with the Danish researcher Jytte Jensen in Aarhus on the Danish role in the research project 'Care Work in Europe' was particularly interesting for this study. (Hansen, Jensen, 2004). This research project – financed by the European Commission – in which six European countries, including Denmark, took part, ran from 2001 to 2005 (Cameron, Moss, 2007). The researcher, Jytte Jensen, allows us access to the preliminary results of the project in Denmark and provides commentary for, among other things, the videos on Denmark that were made within the framework of this project (Korintus, Moss, 2004). In the summer of 2004, we attend a workshop given by Jensen and Korintus on this 'Care Work in Europe' project at the EECERA conference in Malta.

In October 2007, an interview is done with Anders Christensen, who himself had worked as a *pedagog* in a 'forest kindergarten', and had been a teacher for years in a *pedagog institut*. He is the author of numerous publications on the profession of *pedagog* and is, at the moment, working at BUPL as a scientific advisor (Christensen, 2006a; 2006b).

In December 2007 the chief editor of *Børn i Europe* Stig Lundt read the text on Denmark and his remarks were incorporated in the final edition.

5.7.2. The Danish childcare model: no difference between care and education

The first childcare establishments in Denmark were created 180 years ago and consisted, on the one hand, of *Asyler*, institutions for the less fortunate children and, on the other hand, of Fröbel-Kindergarten, for the children from the wealthy families and which had an educational objective. Both types of establishments were merged together as early as 1890 to provide full-time childcare provisions: the so-called *Folkeboernehaven*, that were subsidized by the government in 1919. (Oberhuemer, Ullich, 1997:55; Jensen, Langsted,

2004: 199)[15]. These organisations had an extremely broad view of their task: to care for the children, to provide them with the opportunity to learn, to offer them a safe place while their parents work, to guarantee the health of the children and to discourage social exclusion. With this, Denmark was one of the first countries to abandon the division between 'care and education' in the beginning of the previous century and to choose an approach by which care and education are integrated.

In 1950, there were already 800 centres (childcare centres, kindergartens and out-of-school care). The greatest expansion, however, came in the 1960s when Denmark, just as the other Scandinavian countries, developed the 'Caring state' (Leira, 2006: 30). In 1964, a new law was voted by which the provisions were opened to all children. Starting in the 1970s, the care for young children was, to an ever-increasing degree, entrusted to the national and local governments which financially supported the childcare centres. Leira talks about the 'defamilialisation' of the care for young children. (Leira, 2006:35). Denmark developed into the country with the largest number of government-subsidized provisions for children from 0 to 3 years old (Leira, 2006: 43). As early as 1975, 18% of the 0 to 3-year-olds and 27% of the pre-schoolers in Denmark had a place in childcare. A law dating from 1976 (Bistandsloven) placed the responsibility for the provisions for young children and the out-of-school care with the municipalities.

5.7.2.1. 'Defamilialisation' of the care for young children

The development of a network for the provisions for young children is in keeping with the social-democratic gender-equality political vision in Denmark and the other Scandinavian countries: 'to promote working motherhood and caring fatherhood' (Ellingsaeter, Leira, 2006:267). Cameron and Moss have pointed out that, in many countries, it is the subject of heated political debate concerning how far a state can go in 'defamilialisation' of childcare (Cameron, Moss, 2007: 56). 'The gender equality model presented as predominant in Nordic parenthood policies promotes the parental sharing of both paid and unpaid work and care, and the dual-earner/dual-carer family. This is mainly a model supported by the social democracy and the left. An alternative family model often supported by the centre right, is also evident in policy discourse. This model is formally neutral, valorises unpaid work and care, and advocates making care

---

15 After the First World War, Elise Plasky in Belgium also advocated that childcare should be part of the public education and should be free and accessible to everyone. (Vandenbroeck, 2004: 47).

costless.' (Ellingsaeter, Leira, 2006: 7). This latest model of 'refamilialisation' is, in particular, focused on keeping the role of the family intact and uses, therefore, 'cash benefits for care' strategies: mothers get money from the government to take care of their children at home. Of all the Scandinavian countries, this conservative model was the least popular in Denmark and the cash benefits for childcare was disbanded right after it had been implemented. (Leira, 2006: 41).

Starting in 1984, the care for young children in Denmark was refamilialised in another way by the introduction of parental leave, but only 5% of the Danish fathers took advantage of it. The social democrats felt that this parental leave did not contribute to the promoting of the 'working mothers and caring fathers' and, therefore, in 1997, the social democratic government made the decision to have 2 weeks of the parental leave only available to fathers. The conservative government saw this measure as a restriction of the autonomy of the family and would, in turn, abolish this ruling in 2002. By 2002, Denmark had a place in a childcare facility for 78% of its 0 to 3-year olds and for 94% of its pre-schoolers. (Leira, 2006: 37).

Jensen and Langsted point to the fact that the facilities fall under the auspices of the Ministry of Social Affairs and, based on the Danish Welfare State model, this means that these provisions are intended for all children (and not only the underprivileged, as in other European countries) (Jensen, Langsted, 2004: 200).

At this moment, Denmark is one of the few countries where childcare is a right for all children from the age of 6 months. (Damgaard, 2006:16). In practice, there seems to be a waiting list in a small number of municipalities (10 out of the more than 200 municipalities) (OECD, 2006, 314).

5.7.2.2. The Danish interpretation of professionalism: a unity of care, upbringing and education

Denmark was one of the only countries where, up until 2004, there was no curriculum for kindergarten. (Bennett, 2005). The discussion that arose through the implementation of a curriculum is interesting because, through this, the vision of professionalism in the Danish provisions for young children was brought clearly to the forefront. The intense reactions of the sector against the implementation of this curriculum are striking because it is all about a two-page curriculum that only lays down the most general principles. By comparison, the French curriculum of the *écoles maternelles* consists of 150 pages, the

English curriculum is 128 pages and the Spanish one is 223 pages (Moss, Bennett, 2005: 4-5). On August 1 2004, this 'pedagogical curriculum' was first implemented into the provisions for all children under the age of six. 'The purpose of the pedagogical curriculum is to make the institution 'support, lead, and challenge the learning of children' through among other things 'spontaneous experience and playing' with a focus on children's 'potentials and competences' (OECD, 2006: 315).

The BUPL adopted the attitude of 'constructive criticism', but some educators were vehemently opposed to this curriculum because they experienced this as an infringement on the basic principles of the Danish holistic approach to the child. Many educators feared that learning would become too dominating in the facilities (Lund, 2005: 14).

This controversy about a curriculum (Bennett, 2005: 4-5) can be understood from the perspective of the Danish history of provisions for young children. The facilities for young children were never intended to be a preparation for elementary primary school. In their inception, they interpreted their task very broadly and the aspect of play was particularly important in the tradition of the kindergartens. The Danish early childhood education is characterized not by a focus on learning, as is the case in many European countries, but by relational pedagogy in which interaction is more important than content (Broström, 2005: 5). Teaching is not, in the Danish provisions, seen as a specific activity; it is more a side-effect (Jensen & Langsted, 2004: 198).

The 'pedagogue' does not differentiate between care, upbringing and teaching and the professionalism of the 'pedagogue' encompasses care, child-rearing and teaching. According to Boström, all of this can best be understood in the German concept of *Bildung*. *Bildung* can be defined through the following three criteria:

1) the child's own activity and dialogue with other children

2) a feeling of commitment

3) participation and action (Broström, 2005: 8).

In the law of 1964, there were no guidelines for the pedagogical content of the work of the 'pedagogue'. It was not until 2004 that a curriculum was introduced into the Danish provisions for young children. A number of authors have attempted to find an explanation for the fact that Denmark has been able to achieve a high pedagogical quality in its provisions without there being a clear curriculum for the kindergartens. The high quality of the Danish Early Childhood Education finds its origin in the fact that Denmark spends 2% of its GDP on the care of children between the ages of 0 and 6 years of age. No other country in the world spends more on the provisions for young children (OECD, 2006: 14). The high cost of the Danish provisions has to do with the low pedagogue-child ratio and the high salaries of the pedagogues (OECD, 2006: 313). Both low child-educator ratios and good working conditions, including decent salaries, are important indicators for quality (OEC, 2006: 212 & 216).

Jensen and Langsted are also looking for an explanation for this paradox (the lack of a curriculum and the high pedagogical quality) in the training of the pedagogues.

5.7.3. The generic training for 'pedagogue'

5.7.3.1. The reflective pedagogue

The 'reflective pedagogues' do not, according to Jensen and Langsted, need detailed instructions. Quality has more to do with a strong pedagogical *Ausbildung*, that has also contributed to the fact that a strong sense of professionalism was developed that has given the profession of 'pedagogues' a high degree of social value (Jensen, Langsted, 2004: 206).

Up until 1992, there were three types of educators. The first group, which had existed for more than 100 years, was that of the pre-school worker who worked with children between the ages of 3 and 6. 'Pedagogues' were employed in out-of-school care for children between the ages of 6 and 14. The third group was that of the social 'pedagogues' who worked with children younger than 3 years old and with children and adults with special needs, including residents of care facilities. There was a separate basic education for each of these groups (Jensen, Hansen, 2003).

In 1992, the basic education for the three different professions was integrated into one combined training course that trained for one single profession: that of 'pedagogue' (Oberhuemer, Ulich, 1997: 63).

5.7.3.2. Work terrain of the pedagogue

Due to this reform, the pedagogue has developed into a distinct 'generalist profession' (Cameron, Moss, 2007:144). The pedagogue can use his diploma to find work in a large number of facilities for children, young people, adults with special needs and the elderly.

The pedagogue is the most important attendant in the provisions for young children in Denmark, and he/she is also, at the same time, an excellent example of the far-reaching professionalization of this type of work in the Scandinavian countries. At the moment, there are 90,000 pedagogues in Denmark, good for 3% of the professional population (Jensen, Hansen, 2003). The pedagogues can be employed for people between the ages of 0 and 100. Nearly two-thirds of this group (55,000) works with children younger than 10 year of age in centres for young children (crèches for children up to 3 years of age, pre-schools for children 3 to 5 years old and integrated centres for children from 0 to 5 years old or older), in classes for 6-year olds and in centres for after-school care (*fritidshjem*) connected to a school. In these centres, approximately 60% of the workers are pedagogues and 40% are assistants with a lower diploma (*paedagogmedhjaelpere*).

'Pedagogues' are also employed in youth clubs and other youth work, in residential facilities for children and young people, in residential centres and in daycare centres for handicapped adults and other adults with special needs. These pedagogues can also be found in the function of educational advisor, educational mentors for private childcare workers or as social workers. Pedagogues, therefore, work in an extremely wide variety of pedagogical and social services, but have a strong, specific professional identity. During the past few years, a closer cooperation with the schools has come into being, but the work of the pedagogue remains fundamentally different from that of the teacher, as does the philosophy behind the two professions.

5.7.3.3. The profile of the students

The Danish 'student-pedagogues' form an extremely heterogeneous group with respect to age, gender and ethnic origin. The average age of the first-year students is around 24 years old (Christensen, 2007), which is significantly higher than students who are trained for comparable work in other countries. The Danish students start the course with a certain amount of work and life experience that they have generally gathered as non-qualified assistants in facilities for children. The Danish pedagogue training course is also successful in attracting a relatively high percentage of male students: 8% in the facilities for children between the ages of 6 months and 6 years old and 25% for out-of-school care (OECD, 2006: 313). Students from ethnic minorities have also found their way to the training course. At the moment, they make up about 5% of the student population. (Jensen, Hansen, 2003: 18). For ethnic minorities and refugees, a special 'bridge-building course' has been developed (Jensen, Hansen, 2002: 46). Assistants who have worked with children for several years as non-qualified co-workers have the opportunity to do the course in a shorter period of time.

5.7.3.4. Content of the training course

The Danish Minister of Education has formulated guidelines for the pedagogue training course that involves the structure, the courses, the internships and the exams. Within the common framework, the individual colleges have, however, a large degree of independence with respect to their own programmes. The institutes may, for example, make autonomous decisions concerning the content of subjects and projects, their own teaching methods, reading lists, etc. During the course, a number of disciplines must be dealt with: pedagogy and psychology (together good for 30% of the total curriculum), social and health studies (20%), communication, organisation and management (10%), art and creative subjects, such as native language, music, theatre, arts and crafts, needlework, exercise and physical education and environmental studies (40 %) (Jensen, Hansen, 2004: 45).

The importance of art and the creative subjects in the curriculum demonstrates that great value is placed on the artistic and aesthetic aspects of the work. Alongside of the theoretical subjects, the students must also acquire practical skill in these areas. The schools have special areas and materials for art and creative subjects (workshops, auditoriums, music and physical education classrooms). Foreign visitors are also often amazed by the strong emphasis that is placed on nature and the outdoors in the training course : 'environmental studies' is a separate subject in which students learn how to use outside spaces (playgrounds, forests, beaches,...) in their work.

The internship, which takes a total of 15 months, forms an important part of the course. Students may do a portion of their internship in another country.

The training course for pedagogue can be done in 32 specialised colleges and is the most popular study in Danish higher education. The number of students has, in recent years, risen sharply: from 2,000 enrolments per year in 1992 to 5,500 now. The course takes three and a half years and offers a practically-oriented and, at the same time, strongly theoretically focused programme at the Bachelor level, as do the training courses for teachers, social workers and nurses. The course is free and the students receive, as do all students in Denmark, a stipend of approximately 600 euros per month. This can be augmented with a student loan of 300 euros per month. After completing the course, the childcare workers can continue their studies for a Master's degree in their chosen specialities.

5.7.4. Danish visions and interpretations of professionalism

5.7.4.1. The *pedagogs* themselves develop a model for working with children

In the comparative OECD-PISA study (2001) in which school achievements in the OECD-countries were compared with each other, the Danish children did not perform so well. As a consequence of these poor results, not only was the pressure increased on the students in elementary education, but some even asked if formal education should be started earlier (Lund, 2006: 15). The professional organization of *pedagogs*, BUPL, reacted to this challenge by making the pedagogic vision of the profession of *pedagog* more explicit and by instigating a discussion on the interpretation of professionalism (BUPL, 2006: 7). After consulting the members, the BUPL defined the roles and tasks of the *pedagog* more concretely and, by doing this, endeavors to emphasize the added value of the particular interpretation of professionalism for the children and the community. Alongside of the numerous articles in Danish, an English-language brochure was also published under the editorship of Anders Christensen (BUPL, The work of the pedagogue: roles and tasks).

The fact that, in the Danish provisions for young children, there are no classes[16], the curriculum that was developed is extremely non-specific and there are no pre-determined moments in which prescribed learning activities are planned does not mean, according to the BUPL, that children do not profit from their stay at the centres. 'Many of the activities in the daycare centres challenge the child creatively and physically. The daycare centre is, in a double sense, a social place: it is both a social community for children, but also a social community where children can meet across social distinctions.' (BUPL, 2006: 3). In the BUPL vision, the work of the *pedagog* must be guided by a number of crucial pedagogic principles, but it is the *pedagog* himself who must contextualize these general principles. (BUPL, 2006: 6). The professional expertise of the *pedagogs* is based on personal competencies and on an awareness of one's own norms and values. The expertise of the *pedagog* encompasses both the theoretical and practical knowledge of the development

---

16 Jensen and Langsted point out that, in most countries, the young children are divided into groups according to age, analogous to the class system in education. The Danish form of organization in which one works in mixed age groups, has more in common with the way in which a family functions. (Jensen, Langsted, 2004: 195).

of children, of play and of friendships and conflicts between children. Alongside of this, the knowledge of pedagogical methods and ethical considerations also play an important role in the professionalism of the *pedagog*.

After discussion with *pedagogs* within the BUPL, Christensen developed a model which contains the pedagogical core tasks of the *pedagog* (BUPL, 2007: 8).

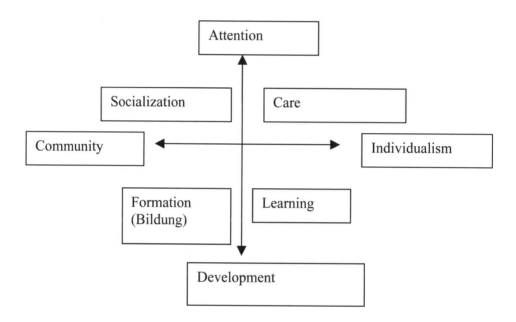

Pedagogical work cannot, according to the Danish pedagogues, be described one-dimensionally because it is multi-dimensional: providing care, socialization in the community, *Bildung* for citizenship and democracy and learning through the development of individual skills. *Pedagogs* do not only make the individual child the central figure, they also emphasize the importance of the community.

Professional caring for children encompasses offering the child a safe environment; in order to do this, the *pedagog* must be conscious of and have empathy for the needs of the child. The *pedagog* must have an eye for the emotional contact and the social interaction with the child, display interest in the child and make it clear that he/she wants to do this and that he/she recognizes and reacts appropriately to the needs of the child. Providing care also means guarding the physical wellbeing of the child by making sure that the child eats, sleeps and plays on time. The *pedagog* must display interest and involvement in what interests the child, listen to his/her questions and try to understand and delve into the child's thoughts and activities. This implies that the *pedagog* has knowledge of and an interest in the current children's culture and the ways in which children express themselves and also that he/she attempts to understand their problems and interests.

Socialization encompasses everything that has to do with how children interact with each other and with the adults in their lives. The essence of socialization is the process by which the individual becomes part of the community. Through contacts with other children and adults, children learn the social codes that are essential for living with each other. 'In the creation of this framework of challenging communities, the pedagogues contribute to ensuring that children are socialized and prepared to get on in social matters throughout life' (BUPL, 2006: 11).

Learning can occur via planned activities, but also, the stimulating of informal learning is one of the tasks of the *pedagog*. Children must be given the opportunity to experiment and investigate through their play, they must be challenged and pass through various learning processes during the time that they attend the centres.

The Danish pedagogues use the concept of *Bildung*, the principle of the German Pedagogy that was developed by Wilhelm von Humboldt (1767-1835). '*Bildung* is the activity of acquisition with which every human being creates his or her worldview. This understanding of *Bildung* implies that it is a lifelong process accompanied by successes and irritations' (Prott, Preissing, 2007:16). *Bildung* must provide children with a framework in order to be able to operate ethically in the society in which they live. Through *Bildung*, children come in contact with knowledge and they learn skills that allow them to develop themselves, to investigate and understand the world around them, to make choices and to take on a set of norms and values. The *pedagog* also has the task to help children, via *Bildung*, to behave in a socially responsible manner and, in doing this, to contribute to the social cohesiveness in society. *Bildung* must ensure that children become active participants in decisions that have to do with citizenship in a democratic society and, thus, participate in promoting solidarity, democracy and humanism in society (BUPL, 2006: 12).

The BUPL model moves in the direction of Oberhuemer's concept of democratic professionalism, where she states that this is based on 'participative relationships and alliances' (Oberhuemer, 2005: 13). The tasks in the BUPL-model that refer to *Bildung* and socialization are then again a concrete interpretation of the vision of Dahlberg, Moss en Pence (1999: 73): 'Early childhood institutions as public spaces or 'forums' situated in civil society in which children and adults participate together in projects of social, cultural, political and economic significance.'

5.7.4.2. The vision of the competent child: constructed and deconstructed

The Danish interpretation of pedagogical professionalism is closely connected to a specific view of the child: the competent child. This view of the competent child is in direct opposition to the view of the immature child as taken from psychoanalysis or developmental psychology. Moreover, the child is not seen as a blank page (*tabula rasa*) onto which adults must 'copy' their knowledge. According to Danish pedagogy, the child is, contrary to this, a co-constructor of his own learning processes (Jensen, Langsted, 2004: 198). 'The concept of the competent child could be conceived of as a part of the Nordic rural tradition, but is also clearly influenced by Rouseau's romantic view of the child' (Brembeck, et al, 2004: 14). The modern view of the competent child has developed historically from the independence of the Scandinavian farm children. This 'farmer's child' was an efficient worker: the girls took care of their brothers and sisters and the boys herded the sheep.

Since the beginning of the 1990's, the notion of the competent child and the specific interpretation of the professionalism of the educator have been on the research agenda. The relationship between children and adults is being discussed and problematized from the perspective of children as 'beings' and 'becomings' (Brembeck, et al, 2004: 18). This gave rise to a new interpretation of the child as a social and cultural being, an active member of society, who provokes, thinks and contributes to his own 'growth' and to the growth of the community. According to Brembeck, Johanssen and Kampmann, a theory about the child was developed in the Scandinavian countries that did not refer to the dual child-adult relationship. 'This new theorizing of childhood was nurtured not only from the universities, but also from professionals in schools and childcare as well as parents. So while the main status of the child as a 'becoming' is its dependence and need for protection, the child as a 'being' takes part in the activities of society on the same terms as adults' (Bremberg, et al, 2004:18).

The construction 'competent child' implies that a child is reasonable, responsible and reflective, that he/she takes responsibility in his own learning process, is a critical and conscious consumer and is capable of taking part in democratic processes, in pupil's councils as well as in family discussions (Brembeck, Johansson en Kampmann, 2004: 22).

According to Gitz-Johansen (2004: 222) there is, however, another side to the coin, namely that the construction of the competent child presupposes that there is also an incompetent child. Ethnic minorities and underprivileged children are, in particular, seen as incompetent, because they do not fit into this Danish image of the child.

'This means that children from ethnic minority backgrounds (as well as low-status social backgrounds) will have to deal with normalizing measures and to assimilate to the pedagogical concept of the 'competent child' (which in practice seems to mean a majority-Danish middle class child) or to face various kinds of marginalization' (Gitz-Johansen, 2004: 223).

Christensen agrees with the Gitz-Johansen analysis, but does not want to go as far as setting up a more structured operation for children of ethnic minorities within the Danish provisions. This would only serve to reinforce the inequality between Danish and minority children (Christensen, 2007: 39:20). He advocates seeking a third path: the assumption of the competent child image and respect for diversity can, according to him, certainly be reconciled in practice. He adds: 'Innovation and fantasy are essential for the Danish system, it would be dangerous to lose that' (Christensen, 2007: 41:02).

5.7.4.3. Pedagogy as co-constructing meaning-making by children and adults

Pedagogy is seen, in the Danish tradition, as the process of being together for children and adults, by which cultural values, such as 'being good to one another' and stretching their capacities or supporting their development with challenges are important elements (Cameron, Moss, 2007: 60).

A Danish pedagogue phrased it as follows: 'A good life, a life with challenges, a life that is worth waking up for. They should be looking forward to the day at the kindergarten or the nursery. We teach the children many different things. We teach them to socialise, they learn about materials, the forest, the world and basically everything. We teach them how to eat food in the proper way, to be friends and to be good to one another' (Korinthus, Moss, 2004: 63). In the Danish film which was made within the 'Care Work in Europe' project, there is a scene that aptly illustrates this vision. A child who is just starting to walk goes out exploring by himself to the area for out-of-school care. In the hall, the toddler meets a group of five 8-year old boys. One of the boys nearly runs the child down, upon which a discussion commences among the boys in which one of the boys explains to the others how you have to deal with toddlers and the boys try to communicate with the child. The toddler looks around proudly and is delighted with all the attention from the 'big' boys. The pedagogue did not intervene to protect the toddler, but observes from a distance.

Via the Sophos method (video-based studies of care and pedagogical practice) of the 'Care Work in Europe' research project (Hansen, Jensen, 2004), it has been determined that the pedagogy in the Danish facilities is much more strongly integrated into the daily activities. 'Ways in which children were conceptualized, for example either as actively involved in creating and leading the events and activities – meaning–makers – or as near-passive recipients of what was on offer seemed to differ. Where children were regarded as meaning-makers, along with staff, and where a high degree of flexibility was actively worked with, the daily 'ingredients' began to take on new dimensions, demanding very active staff involvement and almost constant dialogue, discussion and negotiation' (Cameron, Moss, 2007: 67).

The Danish researchers of 'Care Work in Europe', in the analysis of the meaning-making of the 'pedagogues', differentiated among three types of logic: 'three different institutional sets of logic – school logic, home/family logic and childhood logic' (Hansen, Jensen, 2004: 51). 'The logic appeared to observers by way of number of themes, e.g. principles, intensions, the role of the pedagogue, children-adult relations, views on children, *kropslighed* ('bodyness' or body image) environment and materials' (Hansen, Jensen, 2004: 51). These 'three logics' can be again found in various 'life spaces': 'An organised space of learning with activities controlled by adults; an everyday life space with daily activities such as eating, sleeping, going to the bathroom, walking and the play space, where children define and organize their playing'… '*Kropslighed* refers to how one senses the body, and includes a strong element of sensuousness' (Cameron, Moss, 2007: 75). From the 'Care Work in Europe' study, it appears that the Danish professionals have a different vision of their profession than their Hungarian and English colleagues. They want to allow the children – as co-actors – to have experiences of their own choosing and to make their own discoveries. At the same time, the child is not only regarded as an individual, but also as a member of a community of children and adults. 'The pace is 'chaotic' and involves joy of life, humour, the sound of children, unpredictable and multiple events at the same time' (Cameron, Moss, 2007: 76).

The reactions of the Danish pedagogues to the Hungarian film provide a clear meaning-making of their own professionalism. The Danes felt that the Hungarian video was an example of 'family logic'; the Hungarian childcare staff members had, according to the Danes, an interpretation of professionalism that was based on the replacement of the mother. The Danish (female) pedagogues felt that the Hungarian attitude in the film represented an extremely feminine world. 'The conceptualizing of the everyday life space (in the Hungarian film) was linked to the pace of the day, which was very quiet, calm and predictable. Some (Danish) observers noted that it would be a 'boring workplace' (Cameron, Moss, 2007:76).

The English video attests, according to the pedagogues, on the other hand, to an 'institutional logic, a school rationality controlling the practice' (Cameron, Moss, 2007: 75). As far as the aspect of *kropslighed* is concerned, the Danish pedagogues who took part in the study see a great deal of 'body discipline' in the English video. A great deal of attention is paid to the 'head' and little to the 'body': 'one way or another the body has been reduced to a head in the English film'.

5.7.5. Conclusion: the relevance of the Danish experience

In Denmark and Belgium, after World War I, similar discussions were carried out concerning asylum for young children. According to a number of progressive figures, this should be part of public education. The political government in Belgium did not comply with this demand; the dominant discussion after World War II was the ideology of motherhood and the middle class family (Vandenbroeck, 2004: 55). Denmark made a progressive choice in this debate by being the first country to discontinue the division between care and education for children between the ages of 0 and 6 and by subsidizing childcare. In doing this, Denmark took on the role of pioneer within Europe with respect to the development of a professionalism for the professions dealing with young children and for out-of-school care. Denmark has been able to maintain this pioneering role up through today (OECD, 2006). There is a broad international consensus concerning the fact that 'split systems', in which childcare and kindergarten are separated from each other, enlarge the professionalism problems for the professions dealing with young children (0 to 3-years old) (Oberhuemer, 2005; Vandenbroeck, 2006a; OECD, 2006; Cameron, Moss, 2007).

We have determined, however, that there are those in favor of striving towards a training course at the Bachelor's level. In Flanders, the first signs are now visible of a labor shortage in the professions dealing with young children and the profession itself has to deal with an image that is hardly attractive (Peeters, 2005). As far as this is concerned, the Danish *pedagog* training course can serve as a source of inspiration. The generic character of the course, such that the *pedagog* can be employed in various sectors, is one of the reasons why the training course is extremely attractive to young adults, and has contributed to the high status of the profession in Denmark.

The creative interpretation of professionalism, the importance of artistic subjects, outdoor activities and the co-construction of 'meaning-making' by children and adults in activities that deal with a 'childhood logic' and with daily life, are inspiring aspects for the European early childhood sector.

Within Europe, Denmark has taken this the furthest in the de-familiarization of the education for young children: childcare is a right, and there is a place for 78% of the 0 to 3-year olds. 'Female breadwinning and dual-income earner family structures have become a hegemonic and most likely also an irreversible norm' (Borchorst, 2006: 171). The gender gap concerning the number of hours that are worked outside the home is, in Denmark, small in comparison to other European countries. Most of the mothers in Denmark work full-time (37 hours) (Boje, 2006: 203). This transferring of the tasks of the family to the community was coupled with the development of a pedagogic professionalism that is based on a 'childhood logic'. With this, Denmark has been able to combine a successful gender-equality policy with the development of services for young children and centres for out-of-school care, where children – as 'meaning-makers' actively participate in the creation and steering of situations and activities (Cameron, Moss, 2007: 67).

Denmark can also work as a source of inspiration with respect to the training of non-schooled staff members. Approximately 40% of the staff in the Danish facilities is not trained and they work together with the *pedagogs* who have completed a professional bachelor's degree. After having worked in the 'field' with the *pedagogs* for several years, most of these non-trained staff do a shorter training course that acknowledges their experience as assistant childcare workers. The training course also attracts a high percentage of men and students from ethnic minorities.

In conclusion, the role of the trade union BUPL is interesting in the Danish story. Practically all of the *pedagogs* in childcare centres and out-of- school care are members of the same Union which, alongside of defending the interests of its members, has also played an important role in the upgrading of the professionalism of its members.

6

Conclusion

The analysis of the 'interesting practices and policies' in countries belonging to the EU and to the OECD demonstrates that the integration of childcare (0 to 3 and 4-year olds) into a broader whole in kindergarten (education, New Zealand) or in a system of social pedagogy (Denmark) has given rise to a process of professionalization (the demand for higher education and higher salaries). The professionalization of family day carers, however, remains a problem, even within integrated systems: the educational level and working conditions of the family day carers are lower in comparison to the staff members who work in group care.

A low level of professionalism within group care for the youngest children (0 to 3 and 4-year olds) is inherent in the so-called split systems in which childcare and kindergarten are separate from each other. France is the exception to the rule: the French example of the *éducateur jeunes enfants* demonstrates that it is, indeed, possible to develop a high degree of professionalism within a split system.

Most of the problems concerning professionalism within a split system model can be found in the private commercial childcare sector. However, if commercial daycare centres receive support from the government and/or the business community, it seems that it is then certainly possible to upgrade the professionalism in this 'for profit' sector (New Zealand and The Netherlands).

The professionalization of the organisations thrives in the so-called 'communicative spaces' where researchers, policy-makers and staff work together to develop new knowledge. In all of the countries we studied where a coherent policy has been developed, there is a clear tradition of the sector, the research world and the policy-makers collaborating over long periods of time and in a democratic manner to develop a new type of professionalism. The OECD ascertained that, in countries which were confronted with a policy paradox with respect to professionalism, there was a tendency to set up bachelor-level training courses (OECD, 1997). In all of the countries that we studied – with the exception of the two EC countries of Belgium and The Netherlands – staff members with a bachelor's diploma work with the youngest children (0 to 4-year olds) or initiatives are being taken at the moment to realize this in the near future. These graduates are assisted by lower-schooled personnel who generally have a secondary education. In all of the countries that were studied, there was a process of professionalization, or such a process was being set up such that an investment was being made in the up-grading of qualifications and in better working conditions. Our study has shown that Flanders is counteracting this evolution: for the past 25 years, the Flemish childcare sector has been undergoing a process of deprofessionalization.

Countries which want to introduce the professional with a bachelor's degree, must make a choice between a generic and a specialistic interpretation of professionalism. In countries with a generic model of professionalism – such as Denmark – the assistants carry out the same tasks as the graduates; in countries with a specialistic vision of professionalism, it is chiefly the lower-schooled personnel who take on the care tasks.

The work force in many European and OECD countries consists of approximately one third staff members with a graduate bachelor's degree, one third employees with a secondary level education and one third unschooled personnel. The 'Care Work in Europe' research project has found that a tendency can be observed to give the unschooled employees – via various forms of work-study and the recognition of earlier acquired competencies – the opportunity to move on to abridged training courses in adult education in order to obtain a qualification: 'moving from the current three-tier system in which the third lowest tier (with little or no education) is phased out. This would rule out the possible use of care work as a means of bringing unqualified workers into employment (i.e. care work as a short-term measure to reduce unemployment) unless some way is found of linking education to the requisite level of qualification to the process' (Cameron, Moss, 2007: 145).

The bachelor's training courses in France, Denmark and New Zealand – and in a number of 'Early Years Foundation Degrees' in England – train students to be reflective practitioners who must be capable of constructing practical, new knowledge. Within the training course, *éducateur jeunes enfants*, the method of the *analyse des practiques* is inspiring because it utilizes practical experience to develop new theoretical pedagogical insights. The training course in these countries that we studied is always based on the vision of the competent child. The vision in the *pedagog* training course in Denmark, the teacher training in New Zealand and the course that trains the *éducateur jeunes enfants* leans heavily on the concept of *Bildung*[17], in which each child provides his own interpretation of the world around him and in which the child is able to steer his own learning process. In these countries, we see methods develop in which reflection on the practice steers the learning process (reflective practice cycle, *analyse de pratiques*). In the training courses in France and Denmark, this is taken a step further by also including the mentoring of low-schooled employees in the curriculum of the bachelor's training course. The interpretation of professionalism of the *pedagog* – or the *éducateur jeunes enfants* – encompasses the support of low-schooled assistants in the work-study programme.

In the four countries with a coherent model of professionalism, special opportunities have been created for upgrading the professionalism of those from underprivileged groups. This system works in England via the recognition of achieved competencies within the National Vocational Qualifications system and via the Early Years Sector Endorsed Foundation Degrees. In France, Denmark and New Zealand, unschooled employees from underprivileged groups receive dispensation for relevant practical experience if they take on a more advanced study.

Alongside of the initial training course, the in-service training courses and the continuous work to upgrade one's own professionalism are extremely important (Cameron, Moss, 2007: 145).

The disadvantage of the French system is that the sector within which the *éducateur jeunes enfants* can work is limited (Moss, 2007).

The countries with a coherently developed system of professionalism have invested a great deal in expanding the possibilities for vertical and horizontal mobility within all the professions dealing with young children. The most extensively developed model in this area is the National Qualifications Framework in England that, in theory, offers the possibility to move upward from the lowest level of unschooled jobs to the most highly qualified jobs in Early Childhood Education. However, horizontal mobility is also of essential importance in making the jobs attractive and in avoiding shortages in the labour market in the future. The English model of professionalism, in which one works towards a 'common core' for all professions dealing with children, is one way to make the profession more attractive in the future.

---

17 It has emerged from our study that the Maori concept *Mana* displays strong similarities to the concept of *Bildung*. It is striking that there is no English translation for either of these pedagogical concepts.

Finally, we conclude that being a reflective practitioner presumes a high degree of autonomy. Here we see great differences among the countries we studied. Denmark provides its *pedagogs*, with the largest amount of autonomy; the English system provides limited autonomy and remains strongly controlled by the government. The New Zealand system is extremely inspiring because the *Te Whaariki* curriculum creates a general framework within which each teacher can provide his/her own interpretation.

7

Bibliography

Aballea, F. (1992). Sur la notion de professionnalité. *Recherche sociale,* 124, 39-49.

Adams, P., Vossler, K. & Scrivens, C. (eds.) (2005). *Teachers' work in Aotearoa/New Zealand.* Southbank: Thomson Dunmore Press.

Aelterman, A. (1995). Academische lerarenopleiding. De ontwikkeling van een curriculum-concept als antwoord op maatschappelijke uitdagingen en een verruimde professiona-liteitopvatting. Doctoraal Proefschrift. Universiteit Gent.

Bachelet, P. & Mozère, L. (2004). Die französische école maternelle: Verfrühte Formalisie-rung von Bildungsprozessen? In W. Fthenakis & P. Oberhuemer (ed.), *Frühpädagogik International* (pp. 209-214). Verlag für Sozialwissenschaften: Wiesbaden.

Baeyens, A. (1984). *Uitbouw van de kinderopvang in de Vlaamse Gemeenschap.* Brussel: Ministerie van de Vlaamse Gemeenschap, Administratie voor Gezin en Maatschappelijk Welzijn.

Balaguer, I., Mestres, J. & Penn, H. (1991). *Kwalitatieve Dienstverlening aan jonge kinderen, een discussiedocument.* Brussel: Netwerk Kinderopvang van de Europese Commissie.

Balaguer, I. (2003). Onderwijs voor jonge kinderen in Spanje. *Kinderen in Europa,* in *Kiddo,* 4(7), 20-23.

Barbier, J.-M. (2005). Voies nouvelles de la professionnalisation. In M. Sorel & R. Wittorski, *La Professionnalisation en actes et en questions* (pp. 121-134). Paris : L'Harmattan.

Barbier, J.-M. (2006). Problématique identitaire et engagement des sujets dans les activités. In J.-M. Barbier, E. Bourgeois, G. De Villiers & M. Kaddouri, *Constructions identitaires et mobilisation des sujets en formation* (pp. 15-64). Paris: L'Harmattan.

Barbier, J.-M., Bourgeois, E., de Villers, G. & Kaddouri, M. (2005). *Constructions identitaires et mobilisation des sujets en formation.* Paris: L'Harmattan.

Barnett, R. (1994). The Limits of Competence: Knowledge, Higher Education and Society. Buckingham: Open University Press.

Bennett, J. (2003). Starting Strong, the persistent division between care and education. *Journal of early childhood research,* 1(1), 21-48.

Bennett, J. (2005). Democracy and autonomy get an early start. *Children in Europe*, 5(9), 2-3.

Bertram, T. (2007). *Interview afgenomen door Jan Peeters*. 1 februari. Birmingham.

Bettens, C., Buysse, B. & Stroeykens, H. (2005). Bevraging van onthaalouders aangesloten bij een dienst voor opvanggezinnen in het kader van de evaluatie van hun sociale bescherming. Intern document. Brussel: K&G.

Boje, T. (2006). Working time and caring strategies: parenthood in different welfare states. In A. Ellingsaeter & A. Leira, *Politicising Parenthood in Scandinavia* (pp. 195-216). Bristol: The Policy Press.

Borchorst, A. (2006). The public-private split rearticulated: abolishment of the Danish daddy leave. In A. Ellingsaeter & A. Leira, *Politicising parenthood in Scandinavia* (pp. 101-120). Bristol: Policy Press.

Bosse-Platière, S., Dethier, A., Fleury, C. & Loutre, N. (1995). *Accueillir les jeunes Enfants. Quelles professionnalisation?* Romainville St Agne: Ed. ERES.

Bourdieu, P. (1979). *La Distinction*. Paris: Editions de minuit.

Bourdieu, P. (1992). *Réponses*. Paris : Editions du Seuil.

Bourdoncle, R. (1991). La professionnalisation des enseignants: analyses sociologiques anglaises et américaines, notes de synthèse. *Revue française de pédagogie*, 94, 73-92.

Bourdoncle, R. & Mathey-Pierre, C. (1995). Autour du mot professionnalité. *Recherche et Formation*, 19, 137-148.

Bouzidi, N., Usal, D. & Peeters, J. (1993). *Formation, Insertion et accueil des petits enfants*. Gent: NOW, ACEPP, VBJK .

Boyd, R. (2004). Creating Change - New Zealand's Early Childhood Strategy. In D. Reale, *Learning with other countries: International models of early education and care* (pp. 22-25). London: Day Care Trust.

Brannen, J. & Moss, P. (eds) (2003). *Rethinking Children's Care*. Buckingham: Open University Press.

Brembeck, H., Johansson, B. & Kampmann, J. (eds.) (2004). *Beyond the competent child*. Roskilde: University Press.

Broadhead, P. (2007). *Interview afgenomen door Jan Peeters*. 2 februari. Birmingham.

Broadhead, P. & Aristead, J. (2007). Community partnerships: integrating Early Education with Childcare. *Children & Society*, 21(1), 42-55.

Broström, S. (2005). *Care and education: towards a new paradigm in early childhood education*. Paper presented at the EECERA conference in Dublin.

Brougère, G. & Vandenbroeck, M. (2007). Pourquoi de nouveaux paradigmes? In G. Brougère & M. Vandenbroeck, *Repenser l'éducation des jeunes enfants* (pp. 9-22). Bruxelles: Peter Lang.

BUPL (2006). The work of the Pedagogue: roles and tasks. Copenhagen: BUPL.

Cable, C., Goodliff, G. & Miller, L. (2007). *Developing reflective early years practitioners within a regulatory framework.* Unpublished paper. Milton Keynes: Open University.

Cache (2007). *What is cache,* http://www.cache.org.uk/pdf/whatiscache.pd. 31 januari 2007.

Cadart, M. (2006). *Des parents dans les crèches, utopie ou réalité?* Ramonville Saint-Agne: Erès.

Calder, P. (2005). Barriers to Achieving a Core Graduate Early Childhood Profession in England. Paper presented at the EECERA conference in Dublin.

Cameron, C., Moss P. & Owen C. (1999). *Men in the nursery: Gender and caring work.* London: Paul Chapman Ltd.

Cameron, C. (2001). Promise or problem? A review of the literature on men working in the early childhood services. *Gender, work and organisation, 8*(4), 430-453.

Cameron, C. (2005). Building an integrated workforce for a long-term vision of universal early education and care. Policy Papers N° 3. London: Day Care Trust.

Cameron, C. (2006). Male workers and professionalism. *Contemporary Issues in Early Childhood, 7*(1), 68-79.

Cameron, C. & Moss, P. (2007). Care Work in Europe. Current understandings and future directions. London: Routledge.

Canella, G. (1997). Deconstructing Early Childhood Education: social justice & revolution. New York: Peter Lang.

Carr, M. & Rameka, L. (2005). Weaving an early childhood curriculum. *Children in Europe. 5*(2), 8-9.

Catarsi, E. (2004). Malaguzzi en de revolutie van de gemeentescholen. *Kinderen in Europa,* in *KIDDO, 5*(3), 20-23.

Cheboldaeff, C. (2006). Interview met M . Mony. In M. Mony, Repenser la laïcité à l'aune du respect pour la diversité: Quels dispositifs de formations des professionnels dans l'accueil des jeunes enfants? annex. Lyon: Université Lumières.

Cherrington, S. (2007). *Interview afgenomen door Jan Peeters.* 4 april. Wellington, Nieuw-Zeeland.

Christensen, A. W. (eds). (2006). *Viden og vilje i pædagogers arbejde.* Kopenhagen: BUPL.

Christensen, A. W. (2007). *Interview afgenomen door Jan Peeters.* 25 Oktober. Kopenhagen.

Cochran, M. (1995). European child care in global perspective. *European Early Childhood Education Journal, 3*(1), 61-72.

Cohen, B., Moss, P., Petrie, P. & Wallace, J. (2004). A new deal for Children? Re-forming Education and Care in England, Scotland and Sweden. Bristol: Policy Press.

Cohen, B. (2004). Coming of age in the EU: will children now gain their rights as citizens? *Children in Europe*, 4(4), 6-7.

Coistealbha, S., Peeters, J., De Smul, A. & Usal, D. (1993). *Training and development : a cultural approach.* Gent: NOW, ACEPP, VBJK.

Colley, H. (2006). Learning to Labour with Feeling: class, gender and emotion in childcare education and training. *Contemporary Issues in Early Childhood*, 7(1), 15-29.

Commissie van de Europese Gemeenschappen (2005). *Groenboek 'Demografische veranderingen: naar een nieuwe solidariteit tussen de generaties'.* COM (2005) 94 -16.3.2005. Brussel: Europese Commissie.

Coomans, G. (2002). *Labour supply in European context: Demographic determinants and competences issues.* Presentation at the European Conference on Employment Issues in the Care of Children and Older people. Sheffield Hallam University, 20-21 June.

Council of Ministers of the European Community (1992). *Recommandations on childcare. 21 January. 10258/91.* Brussels: E.C.

Crompton, R. (1987a). Gender and accountancy: a response to Tinker and Neimark. *Accounting organizations and Society*, 12(1), 103-110.

Crompton, R. (1987b). Gender, Status and Professionalism. *Sociology*, 21(3), 421-428.

CWDC (2006). Clear Progression towards an Integrated Qualifications Framework. Leeds: CWDC.

Dahlberg, G., Moss, P. & Pence, A. (1999). Beyond Quality in Early Childhood Education and Care: post-modern perspectives. London: Palmer Press.

Dahlberg, G. & Moss, P. (2005). *Ethics and politics in early childhood education.* London: Routledge.

Dahlberg, G. & Moss, P. (2007). Au-delà de la qualité, vers l'éthique et le politique en matière d'education préscolaire. In G. Brougère & M. Vandenbroeck (eds.), *Repenser l'éducation des jeunes enfants* (pp. 139-164). Bruxelles : Peter Lang.

Dahmani, F. & Hardy, W. (2007). *Hof van Cassatie bevestigt: onthaalmoeder is werknemer.* www.indymedia.be/en/node/9976, 20 december 2007

Dalli, C. (1993). Is Cinderella Back Among the Cinders? A Review of Early 1990s. *New Zealand Annual Review of Education*, 3, 223-252.

Dalli, C. & Cherrington, S. (1994). *Survey of ethical concerns faced by early childhood educators in Aotearoa/New Zealand: preliminary results.* Paper presented to NZARE Conference, Christchurch, New Zealand, December 1-4, 1994.

Dalli, C. & Mitchell, L. (1995). The Early Childhood Code of Ethics: Or how can prise your-self from between a rock and hard place. In *Proceedings of the sixth Early Years Childhood Convention, Vol. 1* (pp. 63-76). Auckland: Tamaki Makaurau.

Dalli, C. (1999). Policies and practice: State of the Arts. In C. Keng (ed.), *Excellence in early childhood education* (pp. 55-69). Subang Jaya: Pelanduk Publications.

Dalli, C. (2002). Being a Early Childhood Teacher: Images of Professional Practice and Professional Identity during the Experience of Starting Childcare. *New Zealand Journal of Educational Studies, 37*(1), 73-85.

Dalli, C. (2003a). *Motherhood, caring and professionalism in family day care: unpacking the debates in family day care.* Paper presented at the 3rd International Family Day Care Conference, 19-23 February 2003. Wellington, New Zealand.

Dalli, C. (2003b). *The challenge/s of professionalism.* Paper presented at the Early Childhood Council Conference, 4th April 200,. Christchurch, New Zealand.

Dalli, C. & Te One, S. (2003). Early Childhood Education in 2002: Pathways to the Future. *New Zealand Annual Review of Education, 12,* 177-202.

Dalli, C. (2005). Pedagogy, collaboration and knowledge: Childcare teachers' reflections on the nature of professionalism. Paper presented at the EECERA conference in Dublin.

Dalli, C. (2006a). Re-visioning love and care in early childhood: Constructing the future of our profession. *New Zealand Journal of Infant and Toddler Education, 8*(1), 5-11.

Dalli, C. (2006b). Redefining professionalism in early childhood practice: a ground-up approach. Views from teachers in care and education settings. *Early childhood folio 10: 2006.* Wellington: Council for Educational Research.

Dalli, C. (2006c). *Reflecting on professionalism in early childhood education: views from New Zealand.* Presentation at the 2nd conference of EC Studies Degrees Network. March 2006.

Dalli, C. (2007). *Interview afgenomen door Jan Peeters.* 4 april. Wellington, Nieuw-Zeeland.

Damgaard, L. (2006). Outsourcing early childhood services. *Children in Europe, 6*(11), 16-17.

Day Care Trust (2004). *A new Era for Universal Childcare?* Policy Papers N°1. London: Day Care Trust.

Dejonckheere, M. & Peeters, J. (2002). Mannen voor kinderopvang, de eerste resultaten. *Vrouwenraad, 3,* 28-36.

Delcroix-Howell, C., Usal, D. & De Smul, A. (1994). *Training, Local Development and Childcare: Evaluation.* Gent: NOW, ACEPP, VBJK.

Deleuze, G. & Guattarri, F. (1980). *Mille Plateaux.* Paris: Editions de minuit.

Deller, J. (1988). *Family Day Care Internationally, a Literature Review.* Ottawa: Queen's Printer for Ontario.

Demuynck, K. & Peeters, J. (2006). *Ouderparticipatie, ook voor vaders.* Gent: VBJK.

Department for Education and Employment (1998). *Meeting the Childcare Challenge.* London: The Stationary Office.

DfES (Department of Education and Skills) (2004a). *Every Child Matters, Change for children.* London: Stationary Office.

DfES (Department of Education and Skills) (2004b). *Every Child Matters, next steps.* London: Stationary Office.

DfES (Department of Education and Skills) (2005). *Ten Years Strategy.* London: Stationary Office.

Dorrance, R. (2007). *Interview afgenomen door Jan Peeters.* 9 januari. London.

Doucet-Dahlgren, A.M. (2004). Accompagner des professionnel(le)s de l'éducation des jeunes enfants dans l'écriture d'un mémoire universitaire. In D. Fablet (ed.), *Professionnel(le)s de la petite enfance et analyse de pratiques* (pp. 67-90). Paris: L'Harmattan.

ECEGO-Expertisecentrum Ervaringsgericht Onderwijs KU Leuven (2007). *Werken aan kwaliteit vanuit het kinderperspectief: welbevinden en betrokkenheid als richtsnoeren. Eindverslag.* Leuven: ECEGO-KU Leuven.

Eheart, B. & Leavitt, R. (1986). Training day care home providers: Implications for policy research. *Early Childhood Research Quarterly,* 1, 119-132.

Ellingsaeter, A. & Leira, A. (2006). *Politicising parenthood in Scandinavia.* Bristol: Policy Press.

Elniff-Larsen, A., Dreylin, M. & Williams, J. (2006). *Employment Developments in Childcare Services for School-age Children.* Dublin: European Foundation for the Improvement of Living and Working Conditions.

Ennals, P. (2007). *Interview afgenomen door Jan Peeters.* 9 januari. London.

Equal Opportunity Commission (2003). *How can suitable, affordable Childcare be provided for all parents who need to work?* www.eoc.org.uk. januari 2007.

Espeel, D. (1987). Bij de minister op de koffie. Interview met Rika Steyaert. *Kido, 1*(1), 9-10.

Esping-Andersen, G. (2002). *Why we need a New Welfare state.* Oxford: Oxford Press.

European Commission Childcare Network (1993). *Men as carers: Report of an international seminar.* Ravenna, Italy, 21-22 May 1993.

European Commission Network on Childcare (1996). A review of Services for Young Children in the European Union 1990-1995. Brussels: EU.

European Commission (1999). *Employment in Europe 1999.* Luxembourg: Office for Official Publications of the European Communities.

European Commission (2001). *Employment in Europe 2001: Recent Trends and Prospects.* Luxembourg: Office for Official Publications of the European Communities.

European Commission (2005a). *Reconciliation of work and private life. A comparative review of thirty European countries.* Brussels: DG for Employment, Social Affairs and Equal Opportunities.

European Commission (2005b). Communications from the Commission on the Social Agenda (COM (2005) 33.final).

European Commission (2006). *Report on equality between women and men.* Brussels: DG for Employment, Social Affairs and Equal Opportunities.

Evans, L. & Davies, K. (2000). No sissy boys here: a content analysis of the representation of masculinity in elementary school reading textbooks. *Sex Roles, 42*(3/4), 225-270.

Everiss, E. (1999). *Bringing it Back to Mind: Two Decades of Family Day Care Development in Aotearoa/New Zealand.* Institute for Early Childhood Studies, Occasional Paper N° 5.

Everiss, E. & Dalli, C. (2003). Family Day Care in New Zealand: Training, Quality and Professional status. In A. Mooney & J. Statham, *Family Day Care, International Perspectives on Policy, Practice and Quality* (pp. 59-77). London-Philadelphia: Kingsley Publishers.

Fablet, D. (ed.) (2004). Professionnel(le)s de la petite enfance et analyse de pratiques. Paris: L'Harmattan.

Farquhar, S., Cablk, L., Buckingham, A., Butler, D. & Ballantyne, R. (2006). *Men at work: Sexism in Early Childhood Education.* Porirua: Childforum Research Network.

Favre, D. (2004). Quelques réflexions de formateur sur l'analyse des pratiques professionnelles en secteur petite enfance. In D. Fablet, *Professionnel(le)s de la petite enfance et analyse de pratiques* (pp. 17-38). Paris: L' Harmattan.

Fédération Nationale des éducateurs de jeunes enfants (2005). *Les XVIèmes Universités d'Automne.* Brochure. Nantes.

Ferri, E. (1992). What makes Childminding work? A Study of Training for Childminders. London: National Children's Bureau.

Fichtelius, M. (1991). Teacher or substitute mother? An account of a worldwide discussion. In J. Peeters, J. Braam & R. Van den Heede, *Family Day Care: teacher or substitute mother* (pp. 138-143). Brussel: VBJK, Kind & Gezin, NOB.

Fisher, J. & Eheart, B. (1991). Family Day Care: a theoretical basis for improving quality. *Early Childhood Research Quarterly, 6,* 549-563.

Foucault, M. (1980). Power/Knowledge: Selected Interviews and Other Writings 1972-1977. London: Harvester.

Freidson, G. (1984). *La profession médicale.* Paris: Payot.

Gabaran, P. (2000). Les EJE en recherche de reconnaissance. *Lien Social,* 516, 6.

Galinsky, E., Howes, C., Kontos, S. & Shinn, M. (1994). *The study of children in family child care and relative care: Highlights of findings.* New York: Families and Work Institute.

Gelder, U. (2003). Carving out a Niche? The work of a Tagesmutter in the New Germany. In A. Mooney & J. Statham, *Family Day Care, International Perspectives on Policy, Practice and Quality* (pp. 41-58). London, Philadelphia: Kingsley Publishers.

Gielen, M. (2004). *From Ghent out into the world.* Amsterdam: SWP.

Gitz-Johanson, T. (2004). The incompetent child: representations of ethnic minority children. In H. Brembeck, B. Johansson & J. Kampmann (eds.), *Beyond the competent child* (pp. 199-228). Roskilde: University Press.

Gooden, A.M. & Gooden, M.A. (2001). Gender representation in notable children's picture books: 1995-1999. *Sex Roles,* 45(1/2), 89-101.

Goris, R. (1994). Kinderopvang op de agenda van Vlaamse Raad. *Kido,* 8(5), 6-7.

Grenel, L. (2000). Ce que sont les éducateur de jeunes enfants. *Lien Social,* 516, 7.

Griffin, S. (1991). A new system of vocational qualifications. In J. Peeters, J. Braam & R. Van den Heede (eds.), *Family Day Care: Teacher or Substitute Mother* (pp. 344-351). Brussel, Gent, Leiden: Kind en Gezin, VBJK, NOB.

Grumet, M.R. (1988). *Bitter Milk: Women and Teaching.* Amherst: University of Massachusetts Press.

Gustavsen, B. (2001). Theory and Practice: the mediating Discourse. In P. Reason & H. Bradbury (ed.), *Handbook of Action Research* (pp. 17-26). London: Sage.

Hansen, H. & Jensen, J. (2004). A study of Understandings in Care and Pedagogical Practice: Experiences using the Sophos Model in cross national studies. Care Work in Europe. Consolidated report.

Harms, T. & Clifford, R. (1980). *Early Childhood Environment rating scales.* New York: Teachers College press.

Harms, T., Cryer, D. & Clifford, R. (1990). *Infant Toddlers Environment rating scales.* New York: Teachers College press.

Hauglund, E. (2005). *Men in Childcare in Norway.* Paper presented at the Men in Childcare Conference. 20 September. National Children's Bureau. London.

Hevey, D. & Curtis, A. (1996). Training to work in the Early Years. In G. Pugh, *Contemporary Issues in the Early Years* (pp. 209-231). Chapman: London.

HM Treasury (2000). Budget 2000: Prudent for a purpose, working for a stronger and fairer Britain. London: The Stationary Office.

H.M. Treasury in conjunction with Department for Education and Skills (DfES), Department for Work and Pensions (DWP), Department for Trade and Industry (dti) (2004). *Choice for Parents, the Best Start for Children: a ten year strategy for childcare.* London: H.M.S.O.

www.surestart.gov.uk/aboutsurestart/strategy/ accessed 21 December 2004.

Hochschild, A.R. (1983). *The managed heart: commercialisation of human feeling.* Berkeley: California Press.

Honge, E. (2003). Free-time for all. *Children in Europe, 3*(4), 4-7.

Hoyle, E. (2001). Teaching, Prestige, Status and Esteem. *Educational Management & Administration, 29*(2), 139-152.

Hughes, P. & Mac Naughton, G. (2000). Consensus, dissensus or community: the politics of parental involvement in early childhood education. *Contemporary Issues in Early Childhood, 1*(3), 241- 257.

Humblet, P. (1998). Analyse et évaluation de la mise en œuvre du programme de l'Œuvre Nationale de L'Enfance pour les milieux d' accueil de jeunes enfants. Thèse doctorale. Bruxelles: Faculté de Médicine, ULB.

Humblet, P. & Vandenbroeck, M. (2008). Sauver l'enfant pour sauver le monde: le «care» et la (re)construction de problèmes sociaux. In G. Brougère & M. Vandenbroeck, *Repenser l'éducation des jeunes enfants* (pp. 189-206). Bruxelles: Peter Lang.

Jensen, J. (1998). Men as worker in Childcare services. In C. Owen, C. Cameron & P. Moss (eds.), *Men as workers in services for young children: Issues of Gender Workforce* (pp. 118-136). London: Institute of Education.

Jensen, J.J. & Hansen, H.K (2002). *Mapping of Care services and the workforce.* Denmark: Care Work in Europe.

Jensen, J.J. & Hansen, H.K. (2003). De Deense opvoeder-begeleider voor alle leeftijden. *Kinderen in Europa*, in *KIDDO, 4*(7), 16-19.

Jensen, J. & Langsted, O. (2004). Dänemark: Pädagogische Qualität ohne nationales Curriculum. In W. Fthenakis & P. Oberhuemer, *Frühpädagogik internatonal, Bildungsqualität im Blickpunkt* (pp. 119-208). Wiesbaden: Verlag für Sozialwissenschaften.

Jobert, G. (1985). Processus de professionalisation et production du savoir. *Education permanente, 80,* 125-145.

Johansson, I. (2003). De nieuwe opleiding tot opvoeder-leerkracht in Zweden. *Kinderen in Europa*, in *KIDDO, 4*(7), 24-26.

Johanssen, K. (2007). Norwegian Department of Education, Personal Communication.

Jones, L. & Osgood, J. (2007). Mapping the Fabricated Identity of Childminders: pride and prejudice. *Contemporary Issues in Early Childhood, 8*(4), 289-300.

Kaddouri, M. (2005). Professionnalisation et dynamiques identitaires. In M. Sorel & R. Wittorski, *La Professionnalisation en actes et en questions* (pp. 145-158). Paris: L' Harmattan.

Karlsson, M. (1996). *Family Day Care in Europe.* European Commission, Employment, Industrial Relations and Social Affairs. DGV/A/3. Brussels: Equal opportunities Unit.

Karlsson, M. (2003). The everyday life of Children in Family Day Care as seen by Carers. In A. Mooney & J. Statham, *Family Day Care, International Perspectives on Policy, Practice and Quality* (pp. 148-162). London, Philadelphia: Kingsley Publishers.

Katz, L. (1985). The Nature of professions: Where is early childhood education? In L. Katz, *Talks with teachers of young children* (pp. 219-235). New Jersey: Ablex Publishing Corporation.

Kind en Gezin (2003). Onderzoek naar en uitwerken van mogelijkheden om de zelfstandige opvangsector te versterken. Plan van aanpak. Intern rapport. Brussel: Kind en Gezin.

Kind en Gezin (2004). Statement van het Strategisch Comité van Kind en Gezin. Brussel: Kind en Gezin

Kunneman, H. (2005a). Voorbij het Dikke Ik: bouwstenen voor een kritisch humanisme. Amsterdam: SWP.

Kunneman, H. (2005b). Social Work as laboratory for Normative Professionalisation. *Social Work & Society, 3*(2), 191-200.

Kyle, I. (2003). Agency and Ethics. Family Day Care Providers' Perspectives on Quality. In A. Mooney & J. Statham, *Family Day Care, International Perspectives on Policy, Practice and Quality* (pp. 129-147). London, Philadelphia: Kingsley Publishers.

Lamb, M.E. (1975). Fathers, forgotten contributors to child development. *Human Development, 18,* 245-266.

Lamb, M.E. (1997). *The role of the father in child development.* New York: John Wiley & Sons.

Leira, A. (2006). Parenthood change and policy reforms in Scandinavia, 1970s-2000s. In A. Ellingsaeter & A. Leira, *Politicising parenthood in Scandinavia* (pp. 27-52). Bristol: Policy Press.

Leitch, R. & Day, C. (2000). Action Research and reflective practice: towards a holistic view. *Educational Action Research, 8*(1), 173-193.

Lequesne, K. (2007). *Personal communication.* 5 december 2007.

Lund, S. (2005). Progress or pitfall? *Children in Europe, 5*(9), 14.

Lyotard, F. (1979). *La condition post-moderne.* Paris: Editions de minuit.

Mac Naughton, G., Rolfe, S. & Siraj-Blatchford, I. (2001). *Doing Early Childhood Research. International perspectives on Theory and Practice.* Crows Nest: Allen & Unwin.

Mac Naughton, G. (2005). Doing Foucault in early childhood studies: applying post-structural ideas. London: Routledge.

Maguire, P. (2001). Uneven ground: Feminism and Action Research. In P. Reason & H. Bradbury, *Handbook of Action Research* (pp. 59-69). London: Sage.

Makkonen, E. (2004). From the Present to Past: discourses of remembered childhoods. In H. Brembeck, B. Johansson & J. Kampmann (eds.), *Beyond the competent child* (pp. 107-126). Roskilde: University Press.

Malaguzzi, L. (1993). Wandelen op zijden draad. *Kinderen in Europa,* in *KIDDO, 4* (3), 14-17.

Malleval, D. (2004). Sensibiliser des éducateur de jeunes enfants en formation à la diversité des pratiques éducatives familiales. In D. Fablet, *Professionnel(le)s de la petite enfance et analyse de pratiques* (pp. 68-110). Paris: L'Harmattan.

Mannaert, N. (2006). *Mannen in een gendergesegregeerde zorgopleiding.* Onuitgegeven scriptie. UGent.

Manning-Morton, J. (2006). The Personal is professional: professionalism and the birth to threes practitioner. *Contemporary Issues in Early Childhood, 7*(1), 42-52.

May, H. & Carr, M. (eds.) (1996). *Implementing Te Whariki: Te Whariki Papers N° 2.* Wellington: Institute for Early Childhood Studies.

May, H. (2002). Early Childhood Care and Education in Aotearoa- New Zealand: An overview of history, policy and curriculum. *McGill Journal of Education,* http://findarticles.com/p/articles/mi_qa3965/is_200201/ai_9046141 14 januari 2008

May, H., Carr, M. & Podmore, V. (2004). Te Whäriki: Neuseelands frühpädagogisches Curriculum 1991-2001. In W. Fthenakis & P. Oberhuemer, *Frühpädagogik International* (pp. 175-189). Wiesbaden: Verlag für Sozialwissenschaften.

Meleady, C. & Broadhead, P. (2002). Diversity: the norm, not the exception. *Children in Europe, 2*(2), 11-15.

Melhuish, E. (2004a). *Child Benefits: the importance of investing in quality childcare.* Policy Papers, No. 9. London: Day Care Trust.

Melhuish, E. (2004b). A literature review of the impact of early years provisions on young children, with emphasis given to children from disadvantaged backgrounds. Report to the Controller and Auditor General. London: National Audit Office.

Menhuir, J. & Hughes, A. (2004). Early Education and Childcare: The Developing Profession. *European Early Childhood Education Research Journal, 12*(2), 21-32.

Meunier, Y. & Chétoui, D. (2002). Les éducateurs de jeunes enfants: une identité professionnelle en évolution? Paris: L'Harmattan.

Meunier, Y. (2004). L'analyse des pratiques en formation initiales d'éducateur de jeunes enfants. In D. Fablet, *Professionnel(le)s de la petite enfance et analyse de pratiques* (pp. 111-132). Paris: L'Harmattan.

Miller, L. (2006). *Developing professionalism in the early years.* Paper presented at the 16th EECERA Conference, Reykjavic, Iceland, August 30th to 2 September 2005.

Miller, L. (2008). Developing New Professional Roles in the Early Years. In L. Miller & C. Cable (ed.), *Professionalism in the Early Years* Hodder: Arnold. In press.

Ministère de l'Emploi et de la Solidarité (2000). *Le Décret « Petite enfance »* n° 2000-762 du 1er août.

Ministère de l'Emploi, de la Cohésion Sociale et du Logement (2005). Diplôme d'Etat d'Educateur de jeunes enfants. Les textes, le métier, la formation, les épreuves de certification. Paris: Berger-Levrault.

Mioche, A. (2005). Profession et professionnalisation: quelques travaux sociologiques fondateur de la notion de profession. In M. Sorel & R. Wittorski, *La Professionnalisation en actes et en questions* (pp. 173-182). Paris: L'Harmattan.

Misplon, S., Hedebouw, G. & Pacolet, J. (2004). *Financiële leefbaarheid van de minicrèches.* Leuven: Hoger Instituut voor de Arbeid.

Mitchell, L. (2002). *Differences between community owned and privately owned early childhood education and care centres: a review of evidence.* NZCER Occasional Paper 2002/2.

Mommen, A. (1979). *De strategie van het politiserend vormingswerk.* Alphen aan de Rijn, Brussel: Samson.

Mony, M. (1993). Insertion professionnelle et qualité de service. In N. Bouzidi, D. Usal & J. Peeters. *Formation, Insertion et accueil des petits enfants* (pp. 28-29). Gent: NOW, ACEPP, VBJK .

Mony, M. (1994). De Franse situatie. In J. Peeters (red.), *Kinderen opvangen kan je leren. 22 standpunten over opleidingen kinderopvang* (pp. 17-20). Gent: VBJK.

Mony, M. (2000). *Histoire des crèches parentales.* Niet gepubliceerde tekst.

Mony, M. (2002). Mal de mère et pieds de marin. In P. Ben Soussan, *Petite Enfance et cultures en mouvement* (pp. 71-90). Rammonville Saint-Agne: Erès.

Mony, M. en Rubio, M. (2002). Ouderinitiatieven in Frankrijk. *Kinderen in Europa*, in KIDDO, 3(7), 15-17.

Mony, M. (2006). Repenser la laïcité à l'aune du respect pour la diversité: Quels dispositifs de formations des professionnels dans l'accueil des jeunes enfants? Lyon: Université Lumières.

Mony, M. (2007). *Interview afgenomen door Jan Peeters.* 2 februari. Birmingham.

Mooney, A. & Statham, J. (2003). *Family Day Care, International Perspectives on Policy, Practice and Quality.* London, Philadelphia: Kingsley Publishers.

Mooney, A. (2003). What it means to be a Childminder, work or love? In A. Mooney & J. Statham, *Family Day Care, International Perspectives on Policy, Practice and Quality.* (pp.111-128). London, Philadelphia: Kingsley Publishers.

Moss, P. (1988). *Childcare and Equality of Opportunity.* Consolidated Report to the European Commission. Brussels: Commission of the European Communities.

Moss, P. (1991a). The European Community: an increasing interest in Childcare. In J. Peeters, J. Braam & R. Van den Heede, *Family Day Care: teacher or substitute mother* (pp. 54-67). Brussel: VBJK, Kind & Gezin, NOB.

Moss, P. (1991b). Day Care for Children in the United Kingdom. In E. Melhuish & P. Moss, *Day Care for Young Children, International Perspectives* (pp. 121-141). London: Routledge.

Moss, P. (ed.) (1995). *Quality targets in services for young children.* Brussels: European Commission.

Moss, P., Owen, C., Statham, J., Bull, J. & Cameron, C. (1995). *Survey of Day Care Providers in England and Wales.* London: Thomas Coram Research Unit.

Moss, P. (ed.) (1996). *A review of Services for Young Children in the EU 1990-1995.* Brussels: European Commission network on Childcare and other measures to Reconcile Employment and Family Responsibilities.

Moss, P. & Petrie, P. (2002). From Children's Services to Children's spaces, Public Policy, Children and Childhood. London, New York: Routledge.

Moss, P. (2003a). Getting beyond Childcare: reflections on recent policy and future possibilities. In J. Brannen & P. Moss, *Rethinking Children's Care* (pp. 25-43). Buckingham: Open University Press.

Moss, P. (2003b). Wither Family Day Care. In A. Mooney & J. Statham, *Family Day Care, International Perspectives on Policy, Practice and Quality* (pp. 234-243). London, Philadelphia: Kingsley Publishers.

Moss, P. (2003c). Wie is de begeleider in de kinderopvang? *Kinderen in Europa,* in *KIDDO,* 4(7), 11-15.

Moss, P. (2004). *A new Era for Universal Childcare.* Policy Papers. No 1. London: Day Care Trust.

Moss, P. & Balaguer, I. (2004). Children, citizens of Europe? *Children in Europe, 3*(7), 3.

Moss, P. (2005). *Learning from other countries.* Policy Papers. No 4. London: Day Care Trust.

Moss, P. (2006). Structures, Understandings and Discourses: possibilities for re-envisioning the early years childhood worker. *Contemporary Issues in Early Childhood, 7*(1), 30-41.

Moss, P. (2007a). *Interview afgenomen door Jan Peeters.* 14 maart. Verona.

Moss, P. (2007b). *Bringing politics into the nursery. Early childhood education as democratic practice.* Working papers in Early Childhood Development 43. The Hague: B. van Leer Foundation.

Moss, P. (2007c). Meetings Across the Paradigmatic Divide. *Educational Philosophy and Theory, 39*(3).

Moyles, J. (2001). Passion, Paradox and Professionalism in Early Years Education. *Early Years, 21*(2), 81-95.

Mozère, L. (1992). Le printemps des crèches. Histoire et analyse d'un mouvement. Paris: L'Harmattan.

Mozère, L. (2007). "Du côté" des jeunes enfants ou comment appréhender le désir en sociologie? In G. Brougère & M. Vandenbroeck (eds.), *Repenser l'éducation des jeunes enfants* (pp. 139-164). Bruxelles : Peter Lang.

Musatti, T. (2007a). *Interview afgenomen door Jan Peeters.* 30 augustus. Praag.

Musatti, T. (2007b). La signification des lieux d'accueil de la petite enfance aujourd'hui. In G. Brougère & M. Vandenbroeck (eds.), *Repenser l'éducation des jeunes enfants* (pp. 139-164). Bruxelles : Peter Lang.

Ndjapou, F. (2007). Paper presented at the international 'Men in Childcare' seminar. 27th of April. Lyon: ESSSE.

Nelson, M. (1990). *Negotiated care: The Experience of Family Day Care providers.* Philadelphia, PA: Temple University Press.

Noddings, N. (1986). *Caring a feminine approach to ethics and moral education.* Berkeley: University of California press.

Noesen, J. (2007). *Interview afgenomen door Jan Peeters.* 26 oktober. Telefonisch.

Noffke, S. (1997). Professional, Personal and Political Dimensions of Action Research. *Review of research in Education, 22*, 305-343.

Oberhuemer, P. & Ulich, M. (1997). Working with Young Children in Europe: Provision and Staff Training. London: Paul Chapman.

Oberhuemer, P. (2000). Conceptualizing the Professional Role in Early Childhood Centres: Emerging Profiles in Four Countries. *Early Childhood Research & Practice, 2*(2), http://ecrp.uiuc.edu/v2n2/oberhuemer.html. 14 januari 2008.

Oberhuemer, P. & Fthenakis, W. (2004). *Früh Pädagogik international*. Berlin: Verlag für Sozialwissenschaften.

Oberhuemer, P. (2005). Conceptualising the Early Pedagogue: Policy Approaches and Issue of Professionalism. *European Early Childhood Education Research Journal, 13*(1), 5-16.

O.E.C.D. (1997). The future of female dominated professions. Paris: OECD.

O.E.C.D. (2000). Country note. ECEC Policy in the Flemish Community of Belgium. Paris: OECD Publications.

O.E.C.D. (2001). Starting Strong. Early Childhood Education and Care. Education and Skills. Paris: OECD Publications.

O.E.C.D. (2004a). *Country note. ECEC Policy in Germany*. Paris: OECD Publications.

O.E.C.D. (2004b). *Country note. ECEC Policy in Ireland*. Paris: OECD Publications.

O.E.C.D. (2006). Starting Strong II, Early Childhood Education and Care. Paris: OECD Publications.

Osgood, J. (2006a). Rethinking Professionalism in Early Years: perspectives from the United Kingdom. *Contemporary Issues in Early Childhood, 7*(1), 1-4.

Osgood, J. (2006b). Deconstructing Professionalism in Early Childhood Education: resisting the regulatory gaze. *Contemporary Issues in Early Childhood, 7*(1), 5-14.

Owen, C. (2003). Men's work? Changing the gender mix of the childcare and early years workforce. Facing the future. Policy Papers No. 6. London: Day Care Trust.

Owen, S. (1989). The unobjectionable service: A legislative history of childminding. *Children and Society, 4*(2), 367-386.

Owen, S. (2003). The development of Childminding Networks in Britain: Sharing the Caring. In A. Mooney & J. Statham (ed.), *Family Day Care. International Perspectives on Policy, Practice and Quality* (pp. 78-92). London, Philadelphia: Jessica Kingsley Publishers.

Owen, S. & Haynes, G. (2007). *Interview afgenomen door Jan Peeters*. 10 januari. London NCB.

Pascal, C. & Bertram, T. (2005). Early Excellence Centres: een model van geïntegreerde zorg. In M. Vandenbroeck (ed.), *Pedagogisch management in de Kinderopvang* (pp. 173-184). Amsterdam: SWP.

Pascal, C. (2007). *Interview afgenomen door Jan Peeters*. 1 februari. Birmingham.

Paul, M. (2004). L'accompagnement: une posture professionnelle spécifique. Paris: L'Harmattan.

Peeters, J., Braam, J. & Van den Heede, R. (1991). *Family Day Care: teacher or substitute mother*. Brussel: VBJK, Kind en Gezin, NOB.

Peeters, J. (1992a). Culturele verschillen in visies op ouderschap en opvoeding in de EG. In A. Holl (ed.), *Opvoedingsondersteuning* (pp. 29-37). Amsterdam: SWP.

Peeters, J. (1992c). Een ethische code voor de kinderopvang. *Kido, 6*(2), 9.

Peeters, J. (1993b). Looking after children? Anyone can do that? L' accueil des enfants, qui le peut? In N. Bouzidi, D. Usal & J. Peeters. *Formation, Insertion et accueil des petits enfants* (pp. 9-15). Gent: NOW, ACEPP, VBJK .

Peeters, J. (1993d). De crèche als plaats om te leren. *Kido, 7*(4), 10.

Peeters, J. & Vandenbroeck, M. (1993). White childcare, multicultural kindergarten. In S. Coistealbha, J. Peeters, A. De Smul & D. Usal, *Training and development: a cultural approach. Formation et développement: l'approche culturelle* (pp. 27-29). Gent: NOW, ACEPP, VBJK.

Peeters, J. (1996). N'importe qui peut-il s'occuper d' enfants? Nouvelles orientations des formations en matière de garde d'enfants en Flandre. *Savoir +, 6,* 85-99.

Peeters, J. (2002). Mannen in de Kinderopvang: noodzakelijke rolmodellen voor jonge vaders. In HIG, *Vaders in soorten* (pp. 233-248). Tielt: Lannoo.

Peeters, J. (2003a). Men in Childcare: An action-research in Flanders. *International Journal of Equality and Innovation in Early Childhood, 1*(1), 72-83.

Peeters, J. (2003b). Kinderopvang als Forum voor de opvoeding van jonge kinderen. In J.R.M. Gerris (ed.), *Opvoeden doen we samen* (pp. 27-32). 's Hertogenbosch: Provincie Noord-Brabant.

Peeters, J. (2004b). Flanders: Improving Inclusion Policies and Services. In D. Reale, *Learning with other countries: International models of early education and care* (pp. 36-39). London: Day Care Trust.

Peeters, J. (2005a). Een noodzakelijke ommezwaai naar duurzaamheid en professionalisering. In M. Vandenbroeck (ed.), *Pedagogisch management in de Kinderopvang* (pp. 51-62). Amsterdam: SWP.

Peeters, J. (2005b). Kinderen en Europa. In M. Vandenbroeck (ed.), *Pedagogisch management in de Kinderopvang* (pp. 32-36). Amsterdam: SWP.

Peeters, J. (2005c). De Beweging van de Oudercrèches in Frankrijk. In M. Vandenbroeck (ed.), *Pedagogisch management in de Kinderopvang* (pp. 168-172). Amsterdam: SWP.

Peeters, J. (2005d). Promoting Diversity and Equality in early childhood care and education-Men in Childcare. In H. Schonfeld, S. O'Brien & T. Walsh, *Questions of quality* (pp. 152-162). Dublin: CECDE.

Peeters, J. (2007a). Including Men in Early Childhood Education: Insights from the European Experience. *New Zealand Research in Early Childhood Education, 10,* 15-24.

Peeters, J. (2007b). De OESO lichtte de Vlaamse Kinderopvang door... *Tijdschrift voor Welzijnswerk, 31*(284), 34-38.

Peeters, J. (2008). Een internationaal perspectief op professionaliteit in de kinderopvang in Vlaanderen. Doctoraal proefschrift. Gent, Universiteit.

Peisner-Feinberg, E. & Burchinal, M. (1997). Concurrent relations between childcare quality and child outcomes: The study of costs, quality and outcomes in child care centres. *Merril Palmer Quarterly, 43*(3), 415-477.

Peisner-Feinberg, E., Burchinal, M., Clifford, R., Culkin, M., Howes, C., Kagan, S. & Yazejian, N. (2001). The relation between Child-Care Quality to Children's Cognitive and Social Developmental Trajectories through second Grade. *Child Development, 72*(5), 15-34.

Penn, H. (2006). Unequal Childhoods : young children's lives in poor countries. London: Routledge.

Petrie, P. (2003). School-age children : services in development. *Children in Europe, 3*(4), 2-3.

Pirard, F. (2005). Cultures de la Qualité des services et cultures de l'accompagnement dans le secteur de l'éducation des jeunes enfants: essai de théorisation. Thèse en vue de grade de docteur en Sciences et l'Education. Université de Liège, Université de Paris Nord 13.

Pirard, F. (2007). *Interview afgenomen door Jan Peeters.* 26 oktober. Telefonisch.

Pirard, F. (2007). L' accompagnement professionnel face aux enjeux de qualité de services. In G. Brougère & M. Vandenbroeck (eds.), *Repenser l'éducation des jeunes enfants* (pp. 139-164). Bruxelles : Peter Lang.

Platière, S., Dethier, A., Fleury, C. & Loutre-Du Pasquier, N. (1996). Les métiers de la petite enfance et la formation continue. *Savoir +, 6,* 51-77.

Pot, L. (1981). Feminisme en kinderopvang. Tegenstrijdige belangen. In NIZW, *Een organisatie van toevalligheden. Liesbet Pot en dertig jaar kinderopvang* (pp. 31-33). Utrecht: NIZW.

Pot, L. (1994). Daar doen ze het zo! Een reisverslag van inspirerende voorzieningen voor jonge kinderen. Utrecht: NIZW.

Preissing C. & Wagner, P. (2003). Kleine Kinder, keine Vorurteile? Interkulturelle und vorurteilsbewusste Arbeit in Kindertageseinrichtungen. Freiburg, Basel, Wien: Herder.

Preissing, C. (2007). *Interview afgenomen door Jan Peeters.* 30 augustus. Praag.

Price, H. (2001). Emotional labour in the classroom: a psychoanalytic perspective. *Journal of Social Work Practice, 2,* 161-180.

Project Voorschoolse Opvang Gent (1984). *Overzicht werking 1979- 1984.* Onuitgegeven rapport. Gent: RUG.

Prott, R. & Preisssing, C. (ed.) (2007). *Bridging Diversity - an Early Childhood Curriculum.* Berlin: Verlag des Netz.

Quintin, C. (1996). La formation continue des professionnels: mythes, mystères et réalités. *Savoir +,* 6, 100-108.

Raad van de Europese Gemeenschap (1992). *Aanbevelingen van de Raad over Kinderopvang.* 21 januari. 10258/91. Brussel.

Rabe-Kleberg, U. (2005). Confidence, control and the market – basic categories of a theory of professional acting. The German example of early childhood education and social change. Paper presented at the EECERA conference in Dublin.

Rinaldi, C. (2005). *In dialogue with Reggio Emilia.* London: Routledge Farmer.

Roggen, T. (2004). Omgangskwaliteit voor orthopedagogen, pleidooi voor een normatieve professionaliteit. Utrecht: Agiel.

Rolfe, H. (2005). *Men in childcare. Working Papers No. 35.* London: Equal Opportunities Commission.

Rorty, R. (1999). *Philosophy and Social Hope.* London: Pinguin Books.

Schön, D. (1983). *The reflective practitioner. How professionals think in action.* London: Temple Smith.

Sciama, S. & Van Turtelboom, Y. (1996). Analyse d'un processus de formation et évolutions des pratiques dans les crèches. *Savoir +,* 6, 100-108.

Sellers, M. & Honan, E. (2007). Putting Rhizomes to work: (E)merging Methodologies. *New Zealand Research in Early Childhood Education,* 10, 145-154.

Sevenhuijsen, S. (1998). Citizenship and the Ethics of Care: Feminist Considerations on Justice, Morality and Politics. London: Routledge.

Simpson, R. (2005). Men in non-traditional occupations: Career entry, career orientation and experience of role strain. *Gender, Work and Organisation,* 12(4), 363-380.

Singer, E. (1993). Kinderopvang: goed of slecht? Een literatuurstudie naar de effecten van kinderopvang. Utrecht: SWP.

Social Ministeriet (1993). *Parental Employment and Caring for Children: Policies and Services in EC and Nordic Countries.* Copenhagen: Danish Ministry of Social Affairs, European Commission.

Somers, A. (1988). Kom in! *Kido,* 2(4), 6-7.

Somers, A. & Peeters, J. (1998). *Diversiteit in de Kinderopvang.* Gent: VBJK.

Sorel, M. & Wittorski, R. (2005). *La Professionnalisation en actes et en questions.* Paris: L'Harmattan.

Spence, K. (2007). Paper presented at the international 'Men in Childcare' Seminar, 27th of April, ESSSE, Lyon.

Stenhouse, L. (1975). An introduction to curriculum research and development. London: Heineman.

Sugar, C.S. (1997). Grounding visual sociology research in shooting scripts. *Qualitative Sociology, 20*(1), 33-55.

Sylva, K., Melhuish, E., Sammons, P., Siraj-Blatchford, I. & Taggart, B. (2004). *The Effective Provision of Pre-School Education Project.* London: Institute of Education.

Taskforce Geïntegreerd Competentiebeleid voor de Kinderopvang (2007). *Een Geïntegreerd Competentiebeleid Kinderopvang voor 2017. Discussienota.* Brussel: Kabinet Welzijn, Kabinet Werk.

Tavecchio, L. (2003). Presentation at the 'Men in childcare' Conference. Ghent, 22 November 2003.

Tavecchio, L. & Fukkink, R. (2005). Dertig jaar empirisch onderzoek naar de Nederlandse kinderopvang. In M. Vandenbroeck (red.), *Pedagogisch management in de kinderopvang* (pp. 114-125). Amsterdam: SWP.

Tobin, J., Wu, D. & Davidson, H. (1989). *Preschool in Three Cultures.* New Haven, London: Yale University Press.

Tobin, J. (2008). Rôle de la théorie dans le mouvement Reconceptualiser l'éducation de la petite enfance. In G. Brougère & M. Vandenbroeck (eds.), *Repenser l'éducation des jeunes enfants* (pp. 139-164). Bruxelles : Peter Lang.

Tronto, J. (1994). Moral Boundaries: a political argument for an ethic of care. Routledge: New York.

Tuominen, M. (1994). The hidden organisation of labour: Gender, race/ethnicity and childcare work in the formal and informal economy. *Sociological perspectives, 37*(2), 229-245.

Urban, M. (2005). Dealing with Uncertainty: Approaching the Dilemma of an Autonomous Early Years' Profession. Paper presented at EECERA conference Dublin.

Urban, M. (2006). Strategies for Change. Gesellschafts- und fachpolitische Strategien zur Reform des Systems frühkindlicher Bildung. Halle: Bertelsmans Stiftung.

Van Ackere, S. (2007). Beleidsbrief Kinderopvang.
http://www.wvg.vlaanderen.be/juriwel/nieuws/beleid/beleidsbrief-0708.htm#P87_2747. 10 januari.

Vandenberghe, L. (1994). Het opleidingsniveau van de medewerkers kinderopvang en de nieuwe kwaliteitsschalen. In J. Peeters (red.), *Kinderen opvangen kan je leren. 22 standpunten over opleidingen kinderopvang* (pp. 28-31). Gent: VBJK.

Vandenbossche, L. (1994). Het standpunt van de minister van onderwijs. In J. Peeters (ed.), *Kinderen opvangen kan je leren. 22 standpunten over opleidingen kinderopvang* (pp. 45). Gent: VBJK.

Vandenbroeck, M. (1991a). Professionalisation. In J. Peeters, J. Braam & R. Van den Heede, *Family Day Care: Teacher or Substitute Mother* (pp. 153-158). Gent: VBJK, NOB, Kind en Gezin.

Vandenbroeck, M. (1991b). Het Europees netwerk kinderopvang, interview met Perrine Humblet. *Kido, 5*(5), 4-6.

Vandenbroeck, M. (1993a). Professionaliteit. In D. Brants, J. Peeters & M. Vandenbroeck, *De School is uit!* (pp. 127-129). Gent: VBJK.

Vandenbroeck, M. & Peeters, J. (1994). A European frame of reference for high quality childcare. In J. Peeters & M. Vandenbroeck (eds.), *Working towards better childcare* (pp. 35-44). Ghent: University of Ghent.

Vandenbroeck, M. (2001). The view of the Yeti. Bringing up children in the spirit of self-awareness and kindredship. The Hague: Bernard van Leer Foundation.

Vandenbroeck, M. (2003). From Crèches to Childcare: constructions of motherhood and inclusion/exclusion in the history of Belgian infant care. *Contemporary Issues in Early Childhood, 4*(2), 137-148.

Vandenbroeck, M. (2004). In verzekerde bewaring. Honderdvijftig jaar kinderen, ouders en kinderopvang. Amsterdam: SWP.

Vandenbroeck, M. & Bouverne-De Bie, M. (2006). Children's Agency and Educational Norms: A Tensed Negotiation. *Childhood, 13(1),* 127-143.

Vandenbroeck, M. (2006a). The Persistent Gap between Education and Care. An 'History of the Present' Research on Belgian Child Care Provision and Policy. *Paedagogica Historica, 42(3),* 363-383.

Vandenbroeck, M. (2006b). *Globalisation and privatisation: The impact on childcare policy and practice.* Working papers in Early Childhood Development, 38. The Hague: Bernard Van Leer Foundation.

Vandenbroucke, F. (2007). *Onderwijsdecreet XVII versterkt kleuteronderwijs en voert CAO's uit.* Website Vice-ministerpresident van de Vlaamse Regering en Vlaams Minister van Werk, Onderwijs en Vorming. 2 februari. http://www.ond.vlaanderen.be/beleid/brief/2007-2008.pdf. 14 januari 2008.

Vandenheede, E. (2006). Gendersegregatie in het onderwijs: jongens in de opleiding 'Kinderzorg'. Onuitgegeven scriptie. Ugent.

van Ijzendoorn, R., Tavecchio, L. & Riksen-Walraven, M. (red.) (2004). *De kwaliteit van de Nederlandse kinderopvang.* Amsterdam: Boom.

Van Keirsbilck, W. (1976). Gespreksnota over de bijscholing van het personeel van de voorschoolse instellingen. Brussel: NCC.

Van Kordelaar, M. (1976). Kinderopvang. Behoeften en problemen. Een evaluatie door verantwoordelijken van onderscheiden kinderopvangvormen. Brussel: CBGS.

Verba, D. (2005). Les mutations dans le métier d'éducateur de jeunes enfants. *Les Enfants dans la ville,* 141, 45-50.

Verba, D. (2006). *Le métier d'éducateur de jeunes enfants.* Paris: La Découverte.

Vereecke, K. (2006). *De Kinderzorg in genderperspectief.* Onuitgegeven scriptie. UGent.

Verhegge, K. (1994). De beoordelingsschalen voor het pedagogisch functioneren in kinderdagverblijven. Brussel: Kind en Gezin.

Verhoeven, J.C., Aelterman, A., Rots, I. & Buvens, I. (2006). Public Perceptions of teachers' status in Flanders. *Teachers and Teaching: theory and practice, 12*(4), 479-500.

Vermeulen, A. (2008). Persoonlijke communicatie. 14 januari.

Verschuur, A. (2007). Professionele opvang gevraagd. Geschiedenis van de Nederlandse Kinderopvang. Den Haag: Stichting Geschiedschrijving Kinderopvang.

Vervaet, V. (1993a). The training of Childcare Worker. La Formation de collaborateur à l'accueil des enfants. In N. Bouzidi, D. Usal & J. Peeters, *Formation, Insertion et accueil des petits enfants* (pp. 16-19). Gent: NOW, ACEPP, VBJK.

VLOR-Vlaamse Onderwijsraad (2002). *Elders verworven competenties.* Leuven, Apeldoorn: Garant.

Vogels, M. (2000). Blauwdruk voor een toekomstgerichte uitbouw van het kinderopvanglandschap in Vlaanderen. Brussel: Ministerie van Welzijn, Gezondheid en Gelijke kansen.

Vogels, M. (2001, 10 mei). *Kinderopvang verdient kwaliteit.* De Standaard, p 8.

Vogels, M. (2002). *Beleidsbrief buitenschoolse kinderopvang.* Brussel: Ministerie van Welzijn, Gezondheid en Gelijke Kansen.

VRT (2006). De Leeuwenkuil. Debat over grenzen van Kinderopvang.

VTM (2002). Recht op Antwoord: debat over grenzen van Flexibele Kinderopvang.

VTM (2006). Recht op Antwoord: debat over Kinderopvang: goed of kwaad.

Wildemeersch, D., Jansen, T., Vandenabeele, J. & Jans, M. (1997). Paradoxen van sociaal leren. Een bijdrage tot de sociaalagogische theorievorming. *Sociale interventie,* 4, 198-208.

Wittorski, R. (2005). Des définitions s'imposent. In M. Sorel & R. Wittorski, *La professionnalisation en actes et en questions* (pp. 183-210). Paris: L'Harmattan.

Woodhead, M. (2007). Le développement du jeune enfant: une affaire de droits. In G. Brougère & M. Vandenbroeck (eds.), *Repenser l'éducation des jeunes enfants* (pp. 139-164). Bruxelles : Peter Lang.

Wohlgemuth, U. (2003). One for all: men on the pedagogue course. *Children in Europe, 3*(5), 22-23.

Colophon

The construction of a new profession
A European perspective on professionalism in Early Childhood Education and Care
Jan Peeters

ISBN 978 90 6665 950 6
NUR 847

Cover photo
Caroline Boudry

Cover design
Lieve Maas Productions, Portland (USA)

Lay out and typesetting
2-D'sign, Hilversum

Publisher
Paul Roosenstein

More information about books of SWP Publishers:
P.O. Box 257, 1000 AG Amsterdam
Internet: www.swpbook.com
Email: swp@mailswp.com